ANTITRUST SIMULATIONS

Second Edition

Steven J. Cernak

Bona Law PC
The University of Michigan Law School
Western Michigan University Cooley Law School

BRIDGE TO PRACTICE SERIES®

WEST
ACADEMIC
PUBLISHING

Bridge to Practice Series® is a trademark registered in the U.S. Patent and Trademark Office.

© 2014 LEG, Inc. d/b/a/ West Academic
© 2020 LEG, Inc. d/b/a West Academic
    444 Cedar Street, Suite 700
    St. Paul, MN 55101
    1-877-888-1330

West, West Academic Publishing, and West Academic are trademarks of West Publishing Corporation, used under license.

Printed in the United States of America

ISBN: 978-1-68467-875-4

To My Parents

ACKNOWLEDGMENTS

The heart of this book is the simulations. All of them arise, directly or indirectly, from experiences I had while working on the General Motors Legal Staff. Those experiences would not have been as plentiful or as enriching if it had not been for the great antitrust lawyers whom I encountered when I joined the Staff straight out of law school: Bob Weinbaum, Bill Slowey and Frank Dunne. They gave me the freedom to fail but the assistance to succeed. In doing so, they continued the General Motors antitrust tradition that included giants such as Tom Leary and Bob Nitschke. They all deserve my thanks.

Other lawyers also encouraged me to think broadly about antitrust issues and lawyer development, such as General Counsels Tom Gottschalk and Bob Osborne. While at General Motors, Chris Johnson supported my first foray into teaching and later, when he became Prof. Johnson, provided me even more teaching opportunities. Greg Curtner and the Schiff Hardin law firm supported those activities as does the Bona Law firm now. I appreciate all the encouragement. Finally, a special thanks to Prof. Danny Sokol, who started me down the academic path with a casual "you'd be a good teacher" remark in an airport several years ago.

Louis Higgins and Prof. Mike Vitiello deserve congratulations for starting this series and making it much easier for professors to ensure their law students graduate ready to practice. They receive my thanks for their positive response when, after seeing an ad for the first books in the series, I requested the opportunity to join in the fun.

Denise Chapman of Schiff Hardin helped me with formatting issues in the first edition and I thank her for her professional assistance. Finally, I must thank the many students in my antitrust classes at The University of Michigan Law School, Wayne State University Law School and Thomas M. Cooley Law School, where I serve or have served as intermittent lecturer or adjunct professor. Their feedback on these "war stories" turned them into the helpful simulations found in this book.

INTRODUCTION

I. *Background*

When I first had the opportunity to teach an advanced antitrust law course at Michigan Law School, I struggled with how to differentiate myself from the professor for whom I was substituting. After all, I was not an academic. I had not authored dozens of law review articles or taught thousands of students or made hundreds of speeches. While I had writing and speaking experience through the American Bar Association Antitrust Section, most of my antitrust practice had been twenty years of applying the antitrust principles I would teach. I decided to use that experience to ensure my students better understood those principles plus how real lawyers applied them and real clients understood them. So all the lectures included practical applications of the principle being discussed and all the exams had nothing but opportunities for students to apply the principles. Judging from the feedback received, the method worked. The success at Michigan was followed by similar success at Wayne State and Cooley. It seemed many students were interested both in the law as well as how that law was applied by real lawyers.

Of course, I was nowhere near the first lawyer or professor who had struggled with how to better prepare law students to be lawyers. Many minds greater than mine have spent much more time worrying about how to teach law students to not only think like lawyers but act like them. The results have been the proliferation of legal practice programs, clinics, practicums, courtroom and counseling competitions and many other ways for law students to "practice before practicing." Fortunately for me, I had that practical experience to teach.

Yet, I thought I could do even more by providing the students the materials necessary to practice real-world antitrust situations. Fortunately again, two events occurred nearly simultaneously. First, Michigan Law School agreed to let me teach a class I called Counseling and Advocacy in Antitrust. The goal of the course was to cover key antitrust principles briefly in typical Socratic method but then provide the students the opportunity to put those principles in practice in one of several realistic settings. While a courtroom argument was one of the simulations, my goal was to show students that, as the course description stated, "antitrust is practiced more often in the boardroom than in the courtroom."

The key for making those simulations as realistic as possible was developing the materials from which the students would be expected to extract the necessary facts to complete their tasks. Perhaps even more than in most areas of the law, antitrust issues and their resolutions are gleaned from reading emails, presentations, articles and other documents and talking to real people. So to make the class as realistic as possible, I created complete documents or excerpts designed to be true-to-life while allowing for several different possible simulations in the classroom. Those twin goals meant that the realism was not perfect—for instance, I did not think it appropriate (or economical) to create enough documents to recreate the weeks-long merger document review process that many antitrust lawyers experience.

The second event was an ad for the Bridge to Practice series that crossed my emails while I was preparing my classroom materials. The textbooks described seemed to be the combination of the documents and speaker notes that I was already preparing for my class. My review of some of the early entries in the series confirmed my suspicions—I could write this textbook just by combining my speaker notes and documents I was preparing for the class anyway. As is often the case in academia, preparation was harder and took longer than I had hoped, in part because I am still practicing antitrust law in addition to teaching it. The result was a chance to "field test" the documents and simulations in classes—these actual fact patterns have been used successfully multiple times—and, I hope, make this text even better for students and professors.

II. Structure of This Book

This book covers the same substantive antitrust topics that all antitrust textbooks cover. It even covers them in the same order used by one of the traditional textbooks that I have used in the past to teach antitrust survey courses. The principles in those substantive areas are illustrated by what I consider to be the key opinions—your professor might choose to add or substitute others. The treatment of each opinion is kept short so that the students will easily pick up the basic points that can then be augmented through class discussions or the simulations. Excerpts of the cases are excluded on the presumption that all students will have easy access to the complete opinions—and also because in practice, nobody excerpts the cases for you.

Each substantive area then contains background information about the simulation for that chapter followed by the documents you will need to better understand the principles and complete the simulation. Depending on the time available, your professor might choose to have you do a simulation for some of the chapters while just discussing the background information for the others. In the Teacher's Manual that accompanies this book, I have suggested several variations on each simulation that your professor might employ. I briefly describe each of them below.

The first chapter covers horizontal restraints, the most dangerous of agreements according to antitrust law, and introduces the fundamental concept of the rule of reason. Some of the classic antitrust cases are covered so that students have the foundation necessary for all lawyers who practice antitrust at all. The background and documents then provide some details of a joint venture between two competing vehicle manufacturers and the steps they have agreed to take to ensure their joint efforts comply with the antitrust laws. Because such compliance programs are a key part of any antitrust counselor's job, the Teacher's Manual describes a simulation in which students would put on a compliance presentation or create a compliance booklet to show to "clients" played by other students. The background and documents might also be used to practice the ways antitrust lawyers review press releases or ask detailed questions to gather the information necessary to evaluate the legality of horizontal agreements.

The second chapter covers the concept of "agreement," a concept that is broader than many unfortunate guilty conspirators over the years might have imagined. The key cases are summarized so you will understand why the concept includes much more than just a written document signed at the end but excludes two competitors just reacting the same way to market events. The difficult cases are very fact-intensive and so the background and documents provide plenty of material about an alleged conspiracy among several competing vehicle manufacturers. The Teacher's Manual describes different ways that you could argue about whether the facts add up to an "agreement," either as jury members or as opposing counsel in oral arguments. Finally, the Manual also describes an exercise where you are given only some of the facts and have the opportunity to unearth more of them by interviewing an employee at your client.

The third chapter covers a variety of antitrust issues that arise in vertical contexts, that is, when a manufacturer sells its products to a retailer or some other reseller. The cases summarized describe how the antitrust treatment of some of these issues, such as price and non-price restraints on retailers, has become much more lenient in recent decades. Price discrimination—selling the same product to different competing resellers at different prices—is also covered. The Teacher's Manual sets up some memo-drafting exercises to give you the opportunity to use the background and documents to advise a client retailer in the world of collectibles. Another potential exercise sets up an initial meeting between counsel for the retailer and the manufacturer of some wildly popular collectibles based on the latest Japanese anime craze.

The fourth chapter deals with the hottest topic in antitrust along with, as of this writing, one of its many open issues. Monopolization, or what actions large and powerful companies should be allowed to take, has become a subject of discussion not just in the legal world but in politics and the mainstream media. The idea that illegal monopolization could be accomplished through price discounts and related tactics has generated a circuit split that the Supreme Court has declined to resolve. The cases summarized cover the first predicate for a successful monopolization claim—is the defendant a "monopolist"—and then move on to the appellate court opinions that discuss when such discounting can be considered illegal "monopolization." The background and documents present an aggressive sales program by a vehicle transmission manufacturer with a high share of a narrowly-defined market. The Teacher's Manual sets up opportunities for you to advise the general counsel of that manufacturer, either in writing or verbally.

The fifth chapter also discusses monopolization cases but the anticompetitive actions considered are varieties of "refusals to deal." The cases summarized again cover the question of "monopolist" but then focus on the limited circumstances when those monopolists must deal with others, usually their competitors. The background and documents describe two competitors in the roadside assistance industry whose cooperative efforts have broken down. The Teacher's Manual has several variations on an opportunity for you as the outside counsel for one of the companies to interact with the company's general counsel before and after negotiating with your counterpart for the other company.

The final chapter covers mergers, a sub-specialty within the antitrust specialty. For reasons explained in the chapter, there are significantly fewer court opinions here than in other areas of antitrust law and the practice has become a regulatory one. The key old opinions are summarized along with one of the few recent ones. The regulatory process and guidelines also are explained. The background and documents concern a proposed merger involving the transmission manufacturer described in the fourth chapter. That material is sufficient to mimic the major aspects of the merger review process. The Teacher's Manual sets up a few variations on a key aspect of that process, the initial meeting between attorneys for the antitrust enforcers and the two merging parties.

Good luck and have fun!

TABLE OF CONTENTS

ANTITRUST SIMULATIONS
Second Edition

CHAPTER 1

HORIZONTAL RESTRAINTS AND AGREEMENTS

I. INTRODUCTION

This chapter explores the antitrust treatment of agreements between competitors, also known as "horizontal agreements." Most such agreements are judged using a "rule of reason" analysis that allows the parties to explain why, on balance, the agreement is pro-competitive and good for consumers. Some such agreements, however, are considered so likely to be anticompetitive that they are considered automatically or "per se" illegal and the parties are not allowed an opportunity to justify them.

The simulation exercise in this chapter gives you an opportunity to: decide if an agreement between two competitors should be judged using the per se or rule of reason analysis; if judged under the rule of reason, determine which aspects of the agreement are necessary or "ancillary" to the pro-competitive aspects of the arrangement; and devise an effective compliance presentation to ensure the client's implementation of the agreement remains legal.

II. AN OVERVIEW OF THE LAW

Antitrust law traditionally has been more concerned about agreements between competitors than agreements between, say, a supplier and a customer. After all, the 19th century "trusts" to which so many people were "anti" were arrangements between competitors. When economists and others draw marketplace arrangements, competitors are usually on the same line or "horizontal" to each other—hence, the term "horizontal agreement." Suppliers are usually drawn above while customers, like distributors or end users, are drawn below; therefore, those arrangements are usually described as "vertical." In almost all circumstances, the same law and basic analysis are applied to both horizontal and vertical agreements. The results, however, can vary considerably and so horizontal and vertical agreements are usually considered separately in antitrust classes.

The original U.S. antitrust law, the Sherman Act passed in 1890, is short and deceptively simple. Its language applicable to all agreements states that "Every contract, combination . . . or conspiracy in restraint of trade or commerce . . . is . . . illegal." 15 U.S.C. 1. Read literally, Section 1's language would prohibit all agreements. After all, an agreement by a steel company to sell to an automobile manufacturer "restrains trade" because the same steel cannot be sold to other car companies. Similarly, a group of lawyers who form a partnership can no longer partner with other lawyers. In 1911's *Standard Oil Co. of New Jersey v. United States*, 221 U.S. 1, the Supreme Court reviewed the common law existing at the time of Sherman Act passage and clarified that Congress meant to prohibit only "undue restraints" under a "standard of reason." So the usual standard in subsequent U.S. antitrust cases has been the "rule of reason," in which the parties to the agreement can justify their actions as, on balance, good for the competitive process and the ultimate consumers.

But not all agreements under Section 1 receive the full "rule of reason" treatment. In *United States v. Trenton Potteries Co.*, 273 U.S. 392 (1927), several competing manufacturers of toilets argued that their agreement on the price each would charge was legal because the agreed-upon price was "reasonable." The Supreme Court decided that the parties were not allowed to argue that the price they fixed was "reasonable" because the mere agreement on <u>any</u> price was anticompetitive and unreasonable. Since then, the case law has evolved to find several categories of horizontal agreements automatically or "per se" illegal: price fixing, supply restrictions, market allocation and boycotts.

The dividing line between horizontal agreements to be analyzed under the rule of reason and those to be analyzed under a per se analysis is not clear. For instance, in *Broadcast Music, Inc. v. Columbia Broadcasting System, Inc.*, 441 U.S. 1 (1979), a group of composers used a trade organization to "fix the prices" at which they would license their songs to users in the form of blanket licenses with flat fees. The Supreme Court used the rule of reason to judge the licenses legal because the product itself—the blanket license—was a pro-competitive way for the composers to license their songs and required some agreement on price to be possible. In most cases alleging agreements to set a certain price or sell only to certain customers, the application of the per se rule is clear and the only question is whether an "agreement" was reached (as explored in Chapter 2).

Parties whose horizontal agreements are challenged under a rule of reason must show that, on balance, the agreement benefits the competitive process and consumers. That showing is easier if the agreement is limited to areas further away from the marketing and sales process. For instance, joint research or production agreements that allow for competition in the sale of the fruits of the agreement usually are found reasonable because the cost savings outweigh any loss of competition in research or production. Even agreements acknowledged to be pro-competitive must avoid secondary agreements that are not reasonably necessary or "ancillary" to the pro-competitive aspects of the arrangement. For instance, in *NCAA v. Board of Regents of University of Oklahoma*, 468 U.S. 85 (1984), the Supreme Court struck down NCAA restrictions on televised football as not ancillary to the organization's otherwise pro-competitive agreements on college football rules.

Justifications for horizontal agreements must focus on the potential effects on competition, not other, non-economic effects. For instance, the Supreme Court rejected the attempt by an engineering association to justify its restrictions on certain competitive bidding practices by its members with claims about their positive effects on quality and safety in *Professional Engineers v. U.S.*, 435 U.S. 679 (1978). Still, the Court has shown some deference to self-regulation, especially by professionals. It created an intermediate mode of analysis between per se and rule of reason, often called "quick look" analysis, for horizontal agreements that are not ancillary to pro-competitive arrangements but also are not obviously anticompetitive. An example and explanation can be found in the Court's review of advertising restrictions by dentists in *California Dental Ass'n v. F.T.C.*, 526 U.S. 756 (1999).

III. BACKGROUND

Grand Motors Corporation is the leading seller of motor vehicles, both globally and in the U.S. Unfortunately for Grand, its sales in the small car segment have been low for years, despite substantial investment in new models. Taylorita Motor Corporation, on the other hand, is an acknowledged expert in the design and manufacturing of small cars. It is the leading seller of such vehicles in the U.S. and the fifth leading seller overall.

Grand and Taylorita have entered an agreement to cooperate on small cars in two ways. First, Taylorita will work with Grand engineers to design and engineer a variant of Taylorita's small vehicle platform for Grand. Second, Taylorita manufacturing engineers will work with their Grand counterparts to help Grand produce the small car in a Grand facility using Taylorita's acclaimed production techniques.

The parties have entered into an agreement that details both aspects of that cooperation. Excerpts of that agreement are included, including the explanatory recitals and the section that outlines the expected compliance efforts of the parties. The parties have also issued a joint press release to explain the cooperation to the public. Finally, Grand currently has two compliance pieces that cover the applicable antitrust principles: one of its "The Right Way" compliance booklets that covers working with competitors; and one of its online "Compliance Series" presentations and tests covering the same topic.

Joint Development Agreement

Grand Motors Corporation, a corporation formed under the laws of the state of Delaware ("Grand") and Taylorita Motor Corporation, a corporation formed under the laws of Japan ("Taylorita") (collectively, "Parties") do hereby enter this agreement to jointly develop vehicles off of Taylorita's Spanner platform so that Grand can manufacture them in its own facility with Taylorita's assistance ("Agreement").

Recitals

WHEREAS Taylorita has begun engineering vehicles off of the next generation of its Spanner platform and those vehicles are expected to be ready to start production in two years;

WHEREAS Taylorita vehicles sold off of the Spanner platform in the U.S. have been the top-sellers in their respective segments in each of the last four years;

WHEREAS Taylorita is concerned that the engineering necessary to meet U.S.-specific safety and fuel economy standards expected to be in force in two years will require significant expenditures by Taylorita;

WHEREAS Grand has vehicle engineering expertise and resources that could be utilized by Taylorita to meet the forthcoming standards;

WHEREAS Grand desires to be able to sell a version of the Spanner in the U.S. so as to improve its performance in the important small vehicle segment;

WHEREAS the Parties believe that spreading the cost of the additional engineering expenses necessary to meet forthcoming U.S. standards over additional Grand vehicles will significantly reduce the per-vehicle expense otherwise expected;

WHEREAS Grand wishes to produce the vehicle itself by converting one of its assembly facilities to processes consistent with Taylorita's small car assembly principles; and

WHEREAS Taylorita is willing to provide manufacturing engineering assistance to Grand as it prepares to and produces the vehicles envisioned by this Agreement (the vehicle development and manufacturing engineering assistance hereinafter known as "the Project"); and

NOW THEREFORE, the Parties enter into this Agreement and hereby agree as follows:

* * * * *

Joint Development Agreement

Section 24. Antitrust Compliance

A. The Parties acknowledge and agree that they remain competitors in the U.S. and globally outside of the Project. Further, they acknowledge and agree that their cooperation under this Agreement will be limited to activities necessary to the successful implementation of the Project.

B. To ensure compliance with all antitrust or competition laws applicable to the Project, the Parties agree that each will develop and implement, at each Party's own expense, an antitrust compliance program. That program will include both initial and ongoing training as reasonably determined by each of the Parties.

C. While the substance of the antitrust compliance program will be determined by each of the Parties, the Parties agree to consult with each other to ensure appropriate consistency between the antitrust compliance programs. The Parties hereby agree that a guiding principle that will be communicated in each Party's antitrust compliance program will be that only employees or representatives of the Party necessary to the successful implementation of the Project will be involved in the Project and have access to the other Party's information. The Parties also hereby agree that each Party will price, market and sell all of its vehicles individually and no information about prices, marketing or sales will be exchanged unless it is necessary to the successful implementation of the Project.

D. The Parties agree that the antitrust compliance program will consist of at least one written (soft or hard copy) set of materials and, at least for Party employees and representatives expected to have regular contact with the other Party, face to face training.

Grand Motors and Taylorita Motor Announce
New Production Joint Venture

Taylorita to help Grand design and build new small car in Grand facility;
2000 jobs saved and new entry made in competitive small car segment.

Detroit, Tokyo—Grand Motors Corporation (Detroit) and Taylorita Motor Corporation (Tokyo) today announce a new production joint venture that will save 2000 U.S. jobs while adding a competitive new entrant to the U.S. small car segment.

Taylorita vehicle and manufacturing engineers will work with their Grand counterparts to create a version of Taylorita's Spanner platform unique to Grand and to be built in Grand's Fontana California assembly plant. The Spanner platform is one of the best-selling passenger car platforms in the world and vehicles sold off it in the U.S. include the Copola small car and SAR4 small sport utility vehicle. The Fontana facility is the only vehicle assembly plant in California and had no announced products once its current product ends production in two years.

"Grand is very excited about the opportunity to work with Taylorita on this project," stated Grand Vice President of Strategic Affairs Zack Smythe. "Not only are we able to keep open the high-quality Fontana facility and learn from Taylorita's widely-acclaimed manufacturing experts, we'll add a great new product to our line-up in a segment where we've traditionally underperformed."

"Teaming with Grand will allow us to spread over a larger volume the engineering costs necessary for the next generation Copola and SAR4 to be sold in the U.S. and Canada," according to Mitsuo Wanatabe, Taylorita's Director of Vehicle and Manufacturing Engineering. "Helping Grand build its version of the vehicle also will give us experience in applying our Taylorita manufacturing principles from Japan and Thailand to the U.S. production market."

Because Taylorita has already begun to engineer several vehicles off the next generation of the Spanner platform, Grand vehicle engineers will be able to join them immediately to help develop a Grand derivative. That vehicle, currently expected to be a small car, is expected to be ready to produce in two years. Simultaneously, a team of Taylorita manufacturing engineers from its Nagoya, Japan assembly plant will spend the next six months in Fontana working with both salaried and represented Grand employees preparing to make the vehicle using Taylorita assembly principles.

The Copola and SAR4 have been the top sellers in the U.S. in their respective segments in each of the last four years. The combination of low prices, high mileage and a fun-to-drive experience has translated well from Taylorita's Japan home to the U.S. market. Grand is the largest seller in the U.S. market but has no entry in the small SUV segment and has never been above fourth place in the crowded small car segment.

The joint venture between the two companies is limited to the engineering and manufacturing of vehicles off this platform. Each company will continue to separately price, market and sell the vehicles developed and manufactured in this joint venture. All other aspects of competition between Grand, the leading seller of motor vehicles in the U.S., and Taylorita, the fifth, will continue.

Contacts:

Grand
Kelly Bommarito
313-556-7712
Kelly.bommarito@grand.com

Taylorita
Grace Shin-Wallace
415-661-6120
Shin-wallaceg@taylorita-usa.com

Grand Success—The Right Way

Competition Law

While all the Grand Success booklets cover legal and regulatory guidelines for succeeding "the right way," this booklet will begin the coverage of the competition or antitrust laws that must be followed. This booklet will cover how we are to act towards and with our competitors. Later booklets will cover our relations with dealers and suppliers.

The competition laws—called antitrust laws in the U.S.—are designed to protect the competitive process so consumers get great products at great prices. The antitrust laws don't protect individual competitors and expect good hard competition that sometimes results in the failure of competitors. The antitrust laws can be complicated and vary by country and the facts. And the penalties can be high, both for Grand and you: Large fines, huge judgments, even jail time are all possible penalties. So while these booklets can't make you an expert, they will highlight the key issues and you should contact the Legal Staff with any questions.

Relations with Grand Competitors

While most antitrust rules are complicated, one is easy: Grand and its competitors cannot agree on prices or any elements of price like discounts and incentives. To make this rule more difficult, "agree" can mean just some discussions with a Grand competitor followed by actions that make it look like that discussion included an agreement. To avoid even that possibility of an "agreement," we should be very careful with any communication with Grand competitors—whether during the business day or on the weekend. And really, we shouldn't be talking price with our competitors at all.

Now clearly, not all communication with competitors leads to a bad agreement and antitrust law understands that fact. But we still must be careful—take a look at these examples:

- Trade associations perform valuable tasks like lobbying on behalf of the industry; however, they are a collection of competitors and so discussions of price, costs and marketing plans must be avoided.

- Product and manufacturing standards can reduce costs and assure the buying public of the safety of the industry's products and procedures—but they can also be used to reduce choice for consumers. Standard setting organizations and trade associations usually have their own rules and even lawyers so Grand employees who participate have to know those rules.

- Benchmarking raises antitrust issues only if done with a competitor. Even then, some benchmarking efforts with competitors can be done if sensitive topics are avoided in various ways.

- Joint ventures, teaming agreements or other strategic alliances with competitors necessarily require close and ongoing communication with the competitor. If the joint effort could lead to positive results for consumers and the communication is limited to only what's necessary to obtain those positive results, the joint effort can be legal under antitrust laws.

All these activities with competitors can be great for consumers and legal under the antitrust laws—but only if done in the right way. So if you think you have a good reason to talk with a Grand competitor, talk to the Legal Staff first—this is one situation where it is much better to seek permission beforehand rather than forgiveness afterwards.

Grand Success—The Right Way (cont.)

Examples

Relations with Grand Competitors

Sharon, Director of Operations at Grand's Customer Assistance Center, met her Frodo Motor Company counterpart for the first time at a recent Call Center Association meeting. The Frodo employee proposed reciprocal tours of their respective U.S. call centers to see how each operates. He also suggested monthly lunches "just to talk over common interests." Finally, he also proposed bringing along his friend, the Frodo Director of U.S. Marketing, and suggested that Sharon bring Grand's Marketing Director to one of the lunches. Sharon is interested in seeing how Frodo's call center operates but is concerned—can she accept any of these invitations?

Sharon's concerns are well-placed. A one-time tour of the operations of each party's call center might be a good, pro-competitive benchmarking exercise that could lead to more efficient operations. Still, it would be a good idea to get an agenda for such a tour down in writing so it would be clear to third parties what happened—and didn't happen. The monthly lunches without agendas or minutes are dangerous. It isn't clear how the discussions could eventually help consumers—and with no records, any future investigators might assume the worst. Finally, the meeting of the respective marketing directors is very dangerous in this context. Sharon should stick to the one-time tour and make sure she properly documents it.

Communications with Competitors

Grand Motors Corporation

Compliance Series

Antitrust Basics

- Antitrust laws protect competition, not competitors
- So important that penalties are large for violations
  - Fines and restrictions
  - Jail time
  - Follow on suits for damages
- This is first in series of online courses

Welcome to this edition of the Grand Compliance Series, online courses and quizzes designed to cover the laws and corporate policies you need to help Grand succeed "in the right way." This course, entitled Communications with Competitors, is the first in a series that will cover what you need to know about the antitrust laws.

The antitrust laws were passed in the 19th century in the U.S. and are designed to protect the competitive process. The thinking is that "free enterprise" works best when it is free of agreements that harm consumers. So the antitrust laws are the "rules of the road" for how Grand can compete in the U.S. There are similar laws outside the U.S., usually called competition laws.

These antitrust laws are considered so important to how our market economy works that the penalties for violating them can be huge. Companies like Grand could end up paying huge fines and be forced to live with restrictions on our activities. Private parties can sue us for damages, which are then tripled. And Grand employees who are involved in the worst kinds of antitrust violations might even go to jail.

The good news is, you don't need to be an expert on all these laws to stay out of trouble. This course will cover the basics that all Grand employees must know—how can we interact with our competitors. Other courses in this antitrust series will cover how we interact with our suppliers and dealers.

Automatic Violations

- Most actions only violate the antitrust laws if all the facts show they are bad for competition
- But some are "per se" illegal
    - Don't get to argue that facts show good for competition
- These actions include agreements with competitors on price, customer allocation or future marketing plans

Under the antitrust laws, most actions Grand can take, either alone or with third parties, are only illegal if all the facts show they are bad for competition and, therefore, consumers. That's why the answer to the question "can we do this" is "it depends on all the facts."

But there are some actions that the antitrust laws have determined are almost always bad for competition. To save time, the courts have said these actions are automatically illegal, no matter what the surrounding facts might be. The fancy legal term for these actions is "per se illegal."

Fortunately, there aren't too many of these "per se illegal" actions. They include agreements with competitors on what price we'll charge; what customers we'll go after; and what our current or future marketing plans are to go after those customers.

"But I Didn't Agree to That..."

- Agreements can be found after communications with others followed by actions that make it look like there was an agreement
- That's why we need to be very careful about communicating with competitors, especially about
  - Prices
  - Costs
  - Marketing Plans

Making it even tougher, a court doesn't have to find a written agreement written by lawyers and signed by the Chairman to find an agreement. Even just some communication followed by action that makes it look like an agreement was made can be enough to find an agreement.

For instance, a discussion between the Grand and Frodo Pricing Directors about how high incentives have been then followed by both companies cutting incentives might be enough to find an agreement—and if so, it will be "per se" illegal and the companies and employees involved will be in big trouble.

That's why we really need to be very careful about any communications outside Grand about topics like all forms of pricing, including incentives and discounts; costs that could reveal what we might be doing soon with prices; and information about how we plan to market and advertise our products. In fact, the best practice is that we shouldn't discuss those topics at all with competitors.

How to Obtain Competitive Information

- We need information about competitors' pricing and marketing in order to compete
- Fine to get that information – but only from sources other than our competitors
  - Dealers
  - Consultants
  - Media
- Make a record of that source so we can explain how we got it, if necessary

Now obviously, Grand needs information about the pricing and marketing plans of our competitors in order to compete with them and offer the right products at the right price to consumers. And antitrust law recognizes that reality.

But the key point is that we should be getting that information from some source other than the competitors. Dealers, consultants, newspapers, websites—all are legitimate sources of such information so long as we don't ask those sources to tell our information right back to our competitors.

To show some future third party, like a government investigator, that we gathered that information appropriately, we should mark down the source right on the document as soon as we obtain the information. A nice test to ensure we properly document such information gathering: If your file was handed to the Wall Street Journal, would it require much explanation to show it wasn't part of an illegal agreement?

"Can I Ever Talk to a Competitor?"

- Other kinds of communications with competitors can be fine under the antitrust laws if done carefully
  - Trade associations
  - Standard-setting organizations
  - Certain joint ventures
- But check in with Legal Staff to make sure

Outside of discussions on price and those other bad topics, there are other interactions that the antitrust laws recognize as good for competition and consumers—but only if done properly. So, for instance, a trade association like the Association of Automobile Manufacturers performs perfectly legitimate and appropriate actions on behalf of many competitive motor vehicle companies, like lobbying. But if AAM meetings are used to fix prices, there would still be an antitrust violation.

Similarly, standard setting bodies can lead to better, safer, less expensive products—but they could also be used to restrict consumer choice. Joint ventures between competitors might lead to more efficient production—but perhaps at too high a price in loss of competition.

So for all these kinds of activities that don't immediately and automatically lead to discussions with a competitor on price, you should check in with the Legal Staff to make sure the activity seems OK and is being run properly.

"Wait . . . You Want Me to Tip Over What?"

- Try to avoid situations where competitors are discussing bad topics like price
  - Whether on Monday in the office or on Saturday on the golf course
- But if you find yourself in a bad situation, leave immediately and in a way that everyone remembers

The safest way to avoid antitrust violations is to minimize contacts with competitors. If you don't need to talk to a competitor, then don't. If you do, then make sure the discussion stays away from topics like price and costs and marketing plans. And remember—to be illegal, the conversations don't have to take place in an office. Many of the worst price-fixing agreements were hatched during social activities like dinners or golfing with competitors.

But in our industry, many Grand employees can't avoid all contact with competitors—and that's fine. But those employees need to take special care to make sure their communications are appropriate and would be seen as appropriate by any third party in the future. And if despite all these precautions, you find yourself in a situation where a competitor is leading the discussion towards prices or other bad topics, you need to get out right away and in a public way that everyone will remember. If you're in a hotel conference room, go ahead and tip over the water pitcher so everyone will remember exactly when you left. Better to be slightly embarrassed now than to be heading to jail later.

Recap and Test

- Certain agreements with competitors are automatically illegal
- Agreements can be found after some communication with competitors
- So avoid all discussion of prices, costs and marketing plans with competitors
- Be careful with all other communications
- Test your understanding on the next pages

Antitrust laws can be complicated, requiring specialized lawyers and economists arguing in front of judges. But the worst antitrust violations are the easiest to understand. Agreements with competitors that fix prices, allocate customers or determine marketing efforts will be automatically illegal.

Agreements can be found even if all that happens is a communication between two competitors followed by actions that make it seem like an agreement exists.

To make sure Grand doesn't stumble into such a bad agreement—and that you don't stumble into jail—avoid all discussions of prices, costs and marketing plans with competitors. For all other communications, make sure you get advice from the Legal Staff before, not after, you start communicating.

Go ahead and test your understanding of the concepts covered by answering the following questions.

Question 1

You are in Grand's pricing department. Your neighbor has a similar job with Frodo. He starts talking about next month's incentives while helping grill up some burgers. You should:

A. Tell him to stop and spill his beer if he doesn't

B. Don't worry about it – you disagree with his opinions anyway

C. Don't worry about it – it's Saturday and nobody will ever know

Here's a situation where a Grand employee is in a sensitive area and happens to know one of his counterparts at a competitor. When the discussion turns to price, what should he do?

A.　This is the correct answer. Turn the discussion away from the bad topics and on to good topics—baseball, weather, anything but our industry. If he doesn't get the hint, make sure to end the conversation in a way that he'll remember.

B.　Wrong. Even if you disagree with his opinion or don't plan to act on the information he provided, you can't control all the actions of both Grand and Frodo's pricing departments. If those departments start moving incentives in the same direction, someone might get suspicious. If an investigation revealed no communication, just two companies reacting to the market in the same way by coincidence, there won't be an antitrust problem. But if the investigation discovers this discussion, then there could be trouble—for Grand and you.

C.　Wrong—it doesn't matter when or how the communication takes place, just that it did. And even if the Frodo employee started the discussion, both of you and your companies can get in trouble. In fact, it is even possible that Frodo and its employee might turn themselves in and receive leniency from the authorities, even if "he started it."

Question 2

You are a Grand battery engineer. A Taylorita battery engineer proposes that the two companies jointly research next generation EV batteries. You should:

A. Tell him no – he's a competitor

B. Tell him yes – joint research is always good

C. Tell him maybe – and go talk to the Legal Staff

Here's an example of a Grand employee who doesn't work on pricing or marketing matters. When a competitor proposes some joint research and development, what should the response be?

A. Wrong. The competitor is not discussing price, costs or marketing plans and so the proposal isn't automatically illegal. It's not automatically legal either so the Legal Staff should be consulted to check it out.

B. Wrong. While the proposal isn't automatically bad, it isn't automatically legal either. Check in with the Legal Staff to see if it is fine and for guidance on how to accomplish it.

C. Correct. Joint research and development often is good for customer and competition and, so, usually is legal under the antitrust laws. But you still need an expert on antitrust law to help make that determination and provide guidance on how to set up the joint effort. Call the Legal Staff to get that guidance—and suggest the Taylorita engineer do the same.

Questions?
Contact Catherine Hudbluh
at
Catherine.hudbluh@grand.
com or any other member
of the Grand Motors Legal
Staff

Grand Motors

CHAPTER 2

AGREEMENT

I. INTRODUCTION

The concept of "agreement" is crucial to Sherman Act Section 1 cases. A Section 1 plaintiff must prove the existence of a "contract, combination . . . or conspiracy" that restrains trade. For actions that are deemed automatically or "per se" unreasonable, only the "agreement" element is left to be proved. Both the concept of "agreement" and the evidence necessary to prove it, however, can be more complicated than they might seem. In some cases, plaintiffs must first show that the entities involved are separate and, therefore, capable of agreeing. In many cases, plaintiffs must show that the actions of the defendants were the result of an agreement and not just simultaneous but independent reactions to identical market conditions. The result of decades of cases is some guiding principles for the courts that must be applied to the facts and market conditions present in the instant case.

The simulation exercise in this chapter gives you an opportunity to: review emails, documents and deposition excerpts in order to debate if the evidence provided is enough for a jury to find an "agreement"; conduct a mock interview of one of the participants to see if all the statements in the documents and deposition excerpts can be drawn out through an interview; and use this evidence, the cases discussed in this chapter and any other cases found in research or assigned by an instructor to conduct a mock summary judgment argument.

II. AN OVERVIEW OF THE LAW

The biggest distinction between Sherman Act Section 1 and Section 2 is the concept of agreement. While the caricature of a smoke-filled room full of top executives shaking hands sometimes actually does occur in antitrust cases, the usual case is not nearly that clear-cut. In particular, courts have dealt with two over-arching legal issues while working through these fact-intensive cases: 1) whether the defendants constitute two or more independent entities capable of conspiring; and 2) whether the evidence is sufficient for a jury to find an agreement.

Whether the defendants represent one entity incapable of conspiring with itself or two or more entities capable of conspiring would seem to be a simple question. That question has been difficult enough, however, to generate multiple pronouncements from the Supreme Court. In *Copperweld Corp. v. Independence Tube Corp.*, 467 U.S. 752 (1984), the Court took on the intra-enterprise conspiracy doctrine and decided that a corporation is incapable of conspiring with its wholly-owned subsidiary. The Court opined that Section 1 was only concerned about the combination of two separate sources of economic power. A parent and its wholly-owned subsidiary, however, have identical economic interests and thus represented only one source of economic power. To rule that one legal entity that controlled another could, nonetheless, conspire would exalt corporate form over the economic substance Congress aimed at in Section 1. Later appellate courts have split when applying *Copperweld's* general language to cases where one defendant owns only a majority interest in another defendant, usually considering whether the ownership interest provides "control."

While the Court provided guidance on when two legal entities might be considered one for Section 1 purposes in *Copperweld*, it later provided guidance on when one legal entity might be considered an agreement among its members in *American Needle, Inc. v. National Football League*, 560 U.S. 183 (2010). The NFL was an unincorporated association of separately owned football teams that owned their own trademarks. The teams, through the NFL, decided to license those marks to other parties to make hats and other souvenirs. The NFL claimed that this licensing action was an act by a single entity—the NFL—and therefore immune from Section 1 challenge. The Court rejected the argument and, again rejecting form for substance, used a "functional analysis" to determine that this arrangement was an agreement among the teams capable of conspiring. As a result, courts must now consider both the level of integration among the defendants, such as trade association members, as well as the subject matter of the agreement to determine if the arrangement constitutes an "agreement" among separate sources of economic power.

Once a court has determined that the defendants are capable of reaching an agreement, it must decide if the evidence is sufficient to allow a jury to find an agreement. While that evidence almost always includes allegations of parallel behavior, the Court has been careful to point out that parallel action, without more, is not enough to prove an agreement. For instance, in *Theatre Enterprises v. Paramount*, 346 U.S. 537 (1954), the Court found there could be no agreement when several defendant movie distributors refused to license showings at a new suburban movie theatre. The defendants denied taking these common actions collusively and showed that it was in each defendant's independent self-interest to deny the license—namely, each would be less profitable replacing a popular downtown theatre with a new suburban one.

More recently, the Court has tried to guide the lower courts with a description of the quantum of evidence necessary to allow a jury to find an agreement. In *Monsanto Co. v. Spray-Rite Service Corp.*, 465 U.S. 752 (1984), the Court said that a finding of "agreement" under Section 1 required "evidence that tends to exclude the possibility of independent action by the [defendants]." In other words, "there must be direct or circumstantial evidence that reasonably tends to prove . . . a conscious commitment to a common scheme." Two years later, in *Matsushita Electric v. Zenith Radio*, 475 U.S. 574, the Court used the following language to state the same principle: "[C]onduct as consistent with permissible competition as with illegal conspiracy does not, standing alone, support an inference of antitrust conspiracy."

Applying these general pronouncements from the Court, lower courts have developed the concept of "plus factors." In cases where the plaintiff asserts an agreement by defendants based on parallel behavior, courts have insisted on the presence of some other "plus factors" to support an inference of concerted action. There is no complete list or ranking of such plus factors; any evidence that "tends to exclude the possibility of independent action" can be used. Some factors, however, have been found powerful by many courts. One example is evidence that the common actions would be in each defendant's self-interest only if all agreed to take them. For instance, defendant sellers reducing supply in the face of rising demand might only make sense for each defendant if all defendants were confident that all would take the same action. Conversely, an allegation of conspiracy that would require irrational behavior from the defendants faces an uphill battle. For instance, the Court in *Matsushita* found the alleged conspiracy not proven because the plaintiff's description of the defendants' behavior—a decades-long agreement among many Japanese electronics manufacturers to keep prices high in Japan and low in the United States so as to drive out American manufacturers and then raise prices to recoup earlier losses—was economically irrational.

The plus factor most often mentioned by plaintiffs is communication among the competing defendants, usually about price, quantity or some other topic on which they have allegedly agreed. Evidence of communication can be ambiguous and is not the strongest "plus factor." After all, much communication among competitors can be competitively benign or even pro-competitive, such as certain standard-setting activities, trade association promotion of the industry and research joint ventures. Communication on certain topics like price and quantities, however, can be much more powerful if followed shortly thereafter by common actions. Courts have not required evidence of a handshake to find an agreement; a "wink and a nod" followed by parallel behavior has been enough. Therefore, antitrust counselors have consistently advised their clients to minimize communication with competitors and, if possible, eliminate any communication on topics like price and quantities that might later form the basis of an allegation of an anticompetitive agreement. When such sensitive information must be exchanged for pro-competitive purposes, such as the evaluation of a potential joint venture or merger, antitrust attorneys put in place procedures to later show that such communication did not lead to an anticompetitive agreement. Finally, antitrust counselors have long advised clients to leave in a memorable way any conversation with competitors that appears headed to dangerous topics. In the classic case of a discussion of price in a smoke-filled hotel conference room, the advice is to "tip over the water pitcher" and leave as soon as possible.

It is not just direct communication, quickly followed by common action, that can lead to successful allegations of agreement. Even indirect communication among competitors can be enough. In *American Column & Lumber v. U.S.*, 257 U.S. 377 (1921), the Court found an agreement where prices of hardwood seemed to move in sync after hundreds of competitors submitted detailed price, sales and inventory information to a trade association who disseminated it to all members. More recently, allegations of agreement have at least survived summary judgment motions where the parallel conduct followed discussion of competitive topics in speeches to industry meetings, media interviews and security analysts earnings calls.

III. BACKGROUND

Grand Motors Corporation is a manufacturer of motor vehicles that sells its products through independent dealers in the United States, Canada and many other countries. All of Grand's competitors—including Frodo, Carizler and Taylorita—use the same distribution method. Each company has a separate network of dealers in each country in which it competes. Each of the manufacturers spends considerable time and money selecting the right number, location and operators of these dealerships. In turn, the dealers invest considerable amounts of their own money in facilities, personnel, inventory and replacement parts. Each of the manufacturers has independently imposed certain vertical restraints on its dealers. These restraints include the requirement to have appropriate facilities and well-trained personnel. All these vertical restraints are designed to provide the consumer with a satisfactory sale and service experience.

One of the vertical restraints that almost all manufacturers, including Grand, Frodo, Carizler and Taylorita, have independently imposed on dealers in all countries for decades is a ban on participation in the "grey market" vehicle market. Grey market vehicles are those originally sold by a dealer in one country—say, Canada—but that eventually are purchased and used in another country—say, the U.S. So long as certain physical changes are made and certifications passed, grey market vehicles are not illegal (that is why they are not "black market" vehicles). These vehicles can, however, confuse consumers and play havoc with a manufacturer's distribution network. Consumers might not understand that some grey market vehicles are not sold in their country and their local dealers might not have the parts or expertise to service them. Manufacturers are upset because of the time and expense they incur to ship what they think is the right mix of vehicles to all parts of the world. Dealers in the country receiving the grey market vehicles are not pleased to lose the opportunity to sell the vehicle originally while still being responsible for its later service. To counter these sales, manufacturers impose penalties, usually financial, on dealers who sell vehicles that later end up in the "grey market."

The flow of grey market vehicles from one country to another usually is not large. When the relationship between the currencies of two countries changes considerably, however, the flow can suddenly increase. For instance, if the Canadian dollar is weak relative to the U.S. dollar, vehicles in Canada might be much less expensive to American buyers than competitive vehicles sold at U.S. dealers. This situation can be exacerbated when companies price their vehicles differently in each country to account for different supply and demand conditions. If the currency and pricing conditions persist for some time, the result can be a large number of vehicles sold by Canadian dealers to American buyers (or to brokers who later resell them to American buyers) and complaints to the manufacturers from dealers on both sides of the border.

Grand, Frodo, Carizler, Taylorita and several of their competitors now face suits in U.S. courts alleging a conspiracy regarding grey market vehicles. The suits have been filed on behalf of both direct purchasers, like dealers, and indirect purchasers, like consumers, and allege violations of Sherman Act Section 1 as well as similar state laws. The suits have survived motions to dismiss and class certification challenges and discovery has been completed.

The classes assert that the defendants agreed to "step up" enforcement of their respective grey market policies and assure one another that the policies would not be abandoned. Such actions allegedly would only make sense if all the manufacturers agreed; otherwise, one defendant could abandon its policies and reap the benefits from additional sales in Canada at the expense of its competitors in the U.S. Also, all the defendants have participated in some calls and meetings in Canada regarding the topic. Some of those meetings included participation by the manufacturers' or the dealers' trade associations or both. Grand has participated in the least amount of communication with its competitors on this subject.

To: Mike Lantesse, Director, Canadian Vehicle Manufacturer Group

From: Jeff Lynch, Frodo Canada Limited General Counsel and Director Industry Relations

Mike—I've got an issue where I think the CVMG can be helpful. It is an industry problem that I think cries out for an industry solution.

As you know, the recent weakening of the Canadian dollar has meant that our Canadian vehicles are suddenly very popular "down south" in the U.S. This happens periodically as the loonie/greenback exchange gets out of whack. Unfortunately, it plays havoc with our distribution on both sides of the border. Brokers buy up our Canadian cars and trucks, especially whatever's hot in the U.S., and then sell them to dealers/brokers/customers in the U.S. It's not illegal, so long as they do the homologation that's necessary—mostly, making sure the speedometers read out in miles per hour and the daytime running lights meet U.S. requirements. A lot of times, those changes aren't made. Or even if they are, the ultimate customer has no idea that the great deal he got on a slightly used or even supposedly new vehicle is really a vehicle that went swimming when it wasn't supposed to. Because it's not illegal but we try to stop it, everybody calls it the grey market.

That's why every manufacturer has some sort of "no export" or even "no sale for resale" clause in its dealer agreement, on both sides of the border. We've had one in our dealer agreements for twenty years and I think Grand's goes back even further. When the U.S./Canadian exchange rate is normal, the provisions just stop the vehicles going overseas, like full size vans to Japan. It really is a customer dis-satisfier when a customer buys a vehicle and then can't get parts or get it fixed. In the U.S./Canada markets, that doesn't happen too much anymore because the lineups are almost the same.

But even if the customer doesn't end up harmed, the dealers in the "receiving" country hate it. So in the U.S. now, our Frodo dealers are screaming that they can't get all the full size pickups they want but there's a Canadian one on the used car dealer's lot across the street—and for a lot less money. And when the U.S. dealers are screaming at the U.S. Frodo sales guys, they start screaming at the FCL guys to "take care" of our dealers. And when we start screaming at the Frodo Canada Limited dealer who sold the truck initially, sometimes they scream back that there's no way for them to know when a customer is just a front for a broker. Sometimes, even we agree that they've been duped. But a lot of times, they're just turning a blind eye to some obvious signs like cash sales or a buyer who's a supposed fleet that we told them was just a front for a broker on our "black list."

Everything that Frodo is experiencing is, I'm sure, going on at Grand, Carizler and Taylorita too. They've got to have vehicles swimming south too and, if so, I'm sure their American bosses are yelling at them too. Seems to me that it would be worthwhile if you could arrange a call with my counterparts at those four companies—I think they all do legal and industry relations too. We could see if there's any interest among them in joining me on some sort of joint solutions—maybe lobbying to make the tax treatment unfavorable? Maybe combining our black lists of suspected exporters? Putting together an industry best practices list to help dealers spot the bad guys? Maybe an education campaign? Anything to slow down the flow of "cheap Canadian cars" and stop the yelling from the American bosses and their dealers.

Let me know if you can arrange. Thanks.

Frodo Canada Limited Official Communication

Dealer Bulletin

XX-98-EN

Steps to Be Taken Regarding Grey Market Vehicles

Grey market vehicles hurt Frodo, our dealers and our customers in both countries,. That is why Frodo has had a long-standing policy prohibiting our dealers in any country from selling for export or selling for resale.

A large and increasing number of Frodo vehicles designed and built for sale and use in Canada have found their way to the United States for sale. Frodo U.S. employees and dealers are upset—and rightly so. We would be upset if the flow of vehicles were going the other way. All these vehicles were first sold by an FCL dealer—and we think all or almost all those sales could have been prevented. This bulletin reminds you about the resources you have to prevent such exports and the steps Frodo is committed to take to help you in this effort.

FCL publishes a "suspected exporter" list and updates it constantly on the dealers-only portion of the Frodo website. You should be familiar with the names and check any prospective customer you do not know against it. If your customer's name is on the list, you should be asking more questions. If you suspect someone is an exporter, let us (and your fellow dealers through the list) know.

FCL also publishes a "best practices" guide. This document has all the learnings from Frodo and our global dealers about how to spot an exporter or a front for an exporter. You should be familiar with this guide and make it a point to incorporate these best practices into your normal business practices. In most cases, there will be no chargebacks to dealers who properly implemented the best practices on a vehicle that still ended up being exported.

Finally, Frodo's Audit Staff will continue to make regular audits of dealers, especially those whose vehicles seem to end up leaving the country most often. If those audits, or other investigations, turn up evidence of an FCL dealer's vehicles being exported, our dealer agreement allows us to chargeback all dealer incentives associated with that vehicle. FCL does not enjoy making such chargebacks but understands they must be done to preserve the integrity of the Frodo distribution system.

Grey market vehicles harm all of us. Please do your part to help eliminate this scourge.

ATTENTION GRAND OF CANADA DEALERS

Dealer Bulletin XX-42-1-EN

Subject: Warranty on Vehicles Originating Outside Canada

Effective with all sales after this bulletin, the following warranty policy will be in place.

During the first 12,500km (7500 miles) and six months after a vehicle is sold in Canada, it must be returned to a Grand of Canada dealer for any warranty service. Any requests for warranty coverage in another country, such as the U.S., will be denied until those limits are crossed. After the thresholds are met, the vehicle may receive warranty service at any Grand dealer in any country.

An identical bulletin is being issued now to Grand dealers in the U.S.

Please contact me or your zone personnel with any questions.

Peter Reesburgh

Dealer Bulletin

Carizler LLC Bulletin to All Carizler U.S. dealers

Bulletin XX-1432

Subject: Change in Warranty Policy

As many of you know from experience, the flow of Canadian "grey market" vehicles has continued to haunt Carizler LLC and our dealers here in the U.S. To help stop that flow and protect the investments made by our dealers everywhere, Carizler announces the following change in warranty policy.

For all vehicles sold after this Bulletin is released, in both the U.S. and Canada, the vehicle warranty will only be honored in the country in which the vehicle was properly sold. Carizler LLC issues the U.S. New Motor Vehicle Limited Warranty while Carizler Canada issues the Canadian version. Carizler's policy has been to honor the warranty in the other country for customer satisfaction reasons. However, the grey market situation makes that policy no longer tenable.

We understand that this policy change to more accurately align with the written warranty might cause some customer confusion as it is implemented. If you have a customer from Canada in your service lane that you think we should take care of, please contact your district sales manager to see if Carizler customer satisfaction policy money should be used in that situation.

As always, thank you for your support as we move forward.

Memo to Carizler Dealers in District 24, Zone 4

From District Manager Michelle J. Ruwinski

Good news for all you great dealers in the greater Denver area! I know some of you have complained about some Canadian grey market vehicles that have made their way down from the "Great White North" to our market. Fortunately, the numbers have not been huge and it doesn't look like any of you, the great Denver dealers, have given into temptation and joined that crowd.

Carizler HQ will be announcing a change in policies to make it even less likely that we'll have to deal with that problem down here. And I believe that HQ and my Canadian colleagues have worked out an "industry solution" to what is clearly an industry problem. More to come.

In the meantime, let's keep working on closing out this month strong. Remember, the current incentive program ends then so let's make the hard close count! I know I can count on you.

Good selling!

MJR

[date]

Note to File

At 10:03am Toronto time on this date, I joined a call arranged by Mike Lantesse of CVMG. Also on the call were Jeff Lynch of Frodo, Pierre Mallard of Taylorita and Steve Rosen of Carizler, all of them being General Counsel and Industry Relations Directors. Mike's invitation said the call was to discuss potential industry solutions to the grey market issue. I was the last one to join the call. I immediately told the group that Grand of Canada could not and would not participate in such calls or meetings with competitors. I told them that we were currently in litigation with a single broker. I did not say but was also concerned about the appearance of trying to affect price in some way. I left the call at 10:07am.

Niall J. Macdougall

[Grand Email]

To: Marc Connote, Grand of Canada Sales Director

Fm: Peter Reesburgh, Grand of Canada Director of Dealer Relations

Re: Summary of Meeting with CVMG, CMVDA, Frodo, Taylorita and Carizler

As requested, here's my summary of the meeting I attended on Grand of Canada's behalf with representatives of the entities listed above.

As you know, the grey market issue continues to generate a lot of noise in the system. While the increase in the number of Grand Canadian vehicles heading south seems to have leveled off, the complaints from American Grand dealers have only increased. We've continued to enforce our forty-year old policy against sales for exports. We haven't upped the penalties or even done any additional audits—but because there were so many grey cars in the last few months, most of our audits find some at every dealer and we just follow our policy and charge them back any incentives we paid on them. We've looked at doing something with warranty but you and I think it would just end up hurting customers and not stopping the flow—we'll see if our Detroit counterparts continue to agree.

Because we've had so many chargebacks, our dealers have gotten upset and sent their organization, the Canadian Motor Vehicle Dealer Association to complain to us. I met with Tim Roon of the CMVDA a couple weeks ago. He freely admits that our Grand policies and enforcement are better and more even-handed than at some of our competitors. But his members are hounding him for some sort of "industry solution" so that they all know what they have to do to avoid the chargebacks.

Tim worked with Mike Lantesse of the CVMG to set up a meeting among the two groups and representatives from us, F, T and C. Niall didn't want anybody from Grand to go but relented when we told him that the CMVDA had called the meeting and there'd be heck to pay if our dealers found out we'd stiffed their organization. So it was agreed that I would go, sort of wave the flag, commiserate with the dealer org guys and, if anything substantive came up, tell the group that Grand thinks the group should get a good competition lawyer to make sure it stays on the right side of the law.

The meeting was downtown at the Fairmont right across from the VIA Rail station. I showed up at 1pm but discovered that the CMVDA was told not to show up until 2pm. Mike Lantesse was there along with all of Niall's counterparts from Frodo, Carizler and Taylorita (can I become an honorary lawyer because of all this?). That first hour, Jeff Lynch from Frodo led the discussion. He seemed really anxious to do something, almost anything, even if it was unlikely to actually accomplish anything. He made several suggestions. First, he suggested that we all combine our "suspected exporter" lists that each of us sends to our dealer body to warn them about brokers. I didn't say anything but I don't want to do it—our list is an "actual exporter" list and I'm much more comfortable about sending our names out to our dealers. Second, he suggested an industry "best practices" list so dealers would know what steps to take that would guarantee them no chargebacks, even if the car later was exported. Again, I remained silent but don't like the idea—I think our best practices list is pretty good and I see no reason to share it with our competitors—and I also don't want to insulate dealers in every situation where they follow the best practices. Finally, he suggested lobbying Revenue Canada to change the tax treatment of the exported vehicles, something about not allowing return of the GST originally paid on the vehicle. That's when I couldn't stay silent anymore. I said that I wasn't here to commit Grand to do anything, only to listen to the CMVDA and that Niall or others would have to weigh in on the other issues and Niall thought the others in the group should get a good competition lawyer.

Mike jumped in and finally took charge of this premeeting. He said that of course nobody was agreeing to anything at this meeting, that any potential agreement would be run by some good competition lawyer and that everyone knew where Grand stood on the issue. We ended up just making small talk—mostly complaining about the Leafs—until Roon from CMVDA showed up.

Timmy made a long speech about how the dealers were paying the penalties for our poor allocation schemes and illogical pricing. Nobody said much of anything until he was done. Then each of us said that we understood that not all dealers are bad, some get duped despite their best efforts and that grey markets cars were bad. Then Timmy asked if we'd be willing to do anything about it, like trying to help dealers understand who the brokers were. He then suggested Lynch's Revenue Canada lobbying and "suspected exporter" list ideas—I think they must have talked beforehand. I jumped in again with the "get a good competition lawyer" remark before Mike could stop me. That seemed to slow down the discussion and we ended up saying that Tim and Mike would have a call next week to see if they could develop next steps. We all shook hands and left about 3:15.

I feel good that we can honestly tell our dealers, if they ask, that we met with their industry representative—but now we can go back to just working with the Grand of Canada dealers ourselves and seeing what their thoughts are rather than the thoughts of Frodo and their dealers.

Let me know if you want to discuss

Reese

[Grand Email]

To: Mike Lantesse, Director, Canadian Vehicle Manufacturer Group

Fm: Niall Macdougall, Grand of Canada General Counsel and Director of Industry Relations

Subject: Re: Industry Meeting

Mike—thanks, nothing more necessary.

NJM

> **To:** Niall Macdougall
>
> **Fm:** Mike Lantesse
>
> **Subject:** Industry Meeting
>
> Niall—Because you were kind enough to allow CVMG, through me, to continue to organize meetings with your counterparts even though Grand has chosen not to participate, I thought it polite to let you know where we stand.
>
> We've had two meetings subsequent to the one with CMVDA that Reese attended for Grand. First, we had a follow up meeting without the dealers about a month later to talk about the possible next steps. Jeff Lynch has a contact at Revenue Canada and said he'd talk with them about the GST issue. He also agreed to get with his guys to see if a common "suspected exporter" list was something Frodo wanted to do. Everyone seemed pretty positive.
>
> Last week, so about a month later, we met again with Tim Roon of the CMVDA. His dealer constituents are still looking for an industry best practices list so they know when they're going to get dinged with a chargeback. We all thought that was pretty ambitious. Jeff reported on his one call with RC—sounded non-committal but not completely negative. No progress yet on the combined blacklist.
>
> I've got detailed minutes if you want to see them. And Timmy really hoped you and Grand would join the next meeting. I respect whatever you decide—just let me know if you need anything more. Thanks.

**Deposition of Niall J. Macdougall
Offices of Gardner, Gervais and Patton
Toronto ON Canada**

[excerpts]

* * *

PLAINTIFF COUNSEL Q: Thank you Mr. Macdougall, now I'd like to move on to this note you wrote to file about your very short call with some of your counterparts, OK?

WITNESS A: Fine with me.

Q: You know the one, I think you have a copy in front of you, is that correct?

A: Yes, the one about the call that began at 10:03. . . .

Q: Yes that's the one.

A: Or that at least I joined at 10:03

Q: Yes, I see you have a copy in front of you and that's good so I can ask you some questions about it

Q: OK

* * *

Q: So now you have joined the call. Did you immediately tell them that you would not participate?

A: Well, not immediately. I said hello to all of them and then launched in to my little speech.

Q: And did you say what you said you said in your note?

A: Yes, I think I used those exact words—we could not and would not participate in calls with competitors on such subjects

Q: Just calls or meetings too?

A: Well I meant both but I'm not sure if I said both.

Q: OK we'll get to meetings in a moment. But why did you make that statement?

A: Well, like I put in the note to file, we had some ongoing litigation at the time with one broker who accused us of tortuous interference with a contract when his customer backed out of a deal.

Q: And was that the only reason you had?

A: Yes, that was the rationale I gave them.

Q: Yes, but did you have any other reason for not wanting to join the call that you did not express to them?

A: Well, yes, as I put in the note, I was concerned that any such call, even if it didn't really have the effect, could leave the impression, really the mis-impression that there would be an effect on price.

Q: OK, I see your sentence in your note to that effect. Can you tell me how you thought a call like this could lead to an effect on price?

A: I said it might lead to that impression, not that it would necessarily actually lead to that effect.

Q: OK, how might such a call lead to that impression?

A: Well, one of the reasons there are grey market vehicles is because the price of the vehicle in Canada is different than the price in the U.S.—or whatever the other country is—and one way, maybe the most effective way, to stop grey market vehicles would be to change the price in Canada.

Q: Raise the price?

A: Yes, raise it so the brokers would not have enough margin to do what they needed to do to sell it in the U.S.

Q: So you were worried about prices—or the impression that prices in Canada might be raised in Canada as a result of these calls?

A: Yes, the impression if lots of other things happened.

Q: OK, were you also worried about a similar impression about U.S. prices?

A: U.S. prices?

Q: Yes.

A: No.

Q: Why not?

A: Well, I sit in Canada and all of us on the phone sit in Canada and we don't know anything about U.S. prices, just that those prices are set by someone else—or at least they are in Grand.

Q: But you weren't worried that stopping the flow of grey market vehicles into the U.S. would reduce the supply of less-expensive vehicles in the U.S. and so increase prices in the U.S.?

A: No, that concoction never crossed my mind until you just said it.

* * *

Q: OK, now when did you write this note to file?

A: Right after the call ended.

Q: Do you always write notes to file after calls with your counterparts from these other companies?

A: No.

Q: Do you ever write such notes in such circumstances?

A: No, I think this is the only one.

Q: Do you ever write such notes when you've had discussions with CVMG?

A: No, again, I think this is the only one.

Q: Is this the only such note to file you've ever written in your Grand career?

A: I can't say "only" but I can't think of another

Q: So what was it about this call that made you do something you've probably never done and write a note to file to contemporaneously memorialize a call?

A: Well, I just didn't have a good feeling about the call and the topic.

Q: You didn't have a good feeling about it?

A: Yes.

Q: Why not?

A: Well, as I wrote down, we were involved in a piece of litigation with a broker already.

Q: Did that litigation with a broker involve only a Grand vehicle or vehicles of some of your competitors?

A: Just a Grand vehicle.

Q: Were any Frodo, Taylorita or Carizler employees involved in any way in the circumstances that led to the litigation with the broker?

A: No, none at all, it was just a Grand case.

Q: And yet you were concerned that this call with representatives of your competitors could somehow affect that litigation?

A: Well, yes.

Q: Concerned enough to do something you'd never done before and write a note to file?

A: Yes.

Q: Could it be that the other reason you wrote down, about the impression that such a meeting could affect price, also made you write the note?

DEFENSE COUNSEL: Objection. You can answer.

A: Well, maybe.

Q: Did that reason help you decide to write down these notes.

A: Yes, probably, I wanted to make sure that I knew what I had said and done.

* * *

Q: After you wrote your note to file, did you tell anyone about the call?

A: Yes, I wanted to make sure nobody else agreed to something by mistake so I told a few folk who often dealt with CVMG and might get a call.

Q: Like Peter Reesburgh?

A: No, but I did tell his boss, Marc Connote.

Q: And did one or both of Messrs. Reesburgh or Connote get such an invitation from CVMG?

A: I don't remember if it was Reese or Marc but, yeah, one of them got a call from Mike Lantesse.

Q: And did they tell you about the invitation before they accepted?

A: Yes, I think we sat down and talked about it.

Q: Did you write them a memo?

A: No, no, I just can't remember if we sat down in person for this one or were on the phone.

Q: And after that meeting or call, did you call Mr. Lantesse back and remind him that you'd said Grand could not and would not participate in such discussions?

A: No, I did not.

Q: Do you know if Messrs. Reesburgh or Connote made a call and delivered such a message?

A: No, I'm sure they did not because we ended up accepting the invitation and sending Reese to the meeting.

Q: Just to be clear, when you say "Reese," you are referring to Mr. Peter Reesburgh, correct?

A: Yes, everyone calls him Reese. I think his wife calls him Reese.

Q: Ok, so none of you made such a call and Mr. Reesburgh ended up attending the meeting—why, given your "little speech" in which you said Grand would not attend such CVMG meetings on this topic, did you allow him to attend this one?

A: Well, we were a little hesitant but we understood, you know, at the time, that it was really a CMVDA meeting and we thought it would be helpful for Reese, our dealer relations director, to go to such a meeting called by the most important dealer association.

Q: Why was it important for him to go to this meeting?

A: Well, our dealers were not happy with what they thought were a lot of chargebacks and they'd told us that and we didn't want to make it seem like we didn't care about their concerns.

Q: But you—that is, someone from Grand—had already met with some Grand dealers about their concerns regarding chargebacks for grey market vehicles?

A: Yes, it was Reese for sure, maybe Marc too, but they met with a few Grand dealers plus Tim Roon from CMVDA and listened to their complaints.

Q: So if you'd already heard the complaints from CMVDA and some Grand dealers, why did you need to go to this meeting along with representatives of your competitors?

A: Well, we didn't need to go but we thought if we didn't go, CMVDA could imply to dealers from our absence that we didn't care about their concerns.

34

Q: But if that happened, then you could just remind them about your earlier Grand dealers only meeting with CMVDA, couldn't you?

A: Yes we could but it would be better—well, better for dealer relations—not to have to answer such a question just by showing up and, you know, waving the Grand flag.

Q: Did you know that CMVDA was told not to show up until an hour after the scheduled start time?

A: No, I did not.

Q: Do you know if the invitation came from CMVDA or CVMG?

A: I'm not sure which made the first invitation but I remember both ended up talking to Reese and Marc about the meeting.

Q: So it wasn't just CMVDA, the dealer organization, who was encouraging you to attend?

A: No, it was both of them.

* * *

Q: Now I'd like to refer you to notes about the meeting that Mr. Reesburgh sent to Mr. Connote shortly after the meeting. I think you have a copy of that email in front of you, is that correct?

A: Yes, I see them here.

Q: First, did you receive a copy of this email?

A: Not at the time, or not that I remembered, not before I was preparing for today.

Q: OK, do you see the part of a sentence that I highlighted that says Mr. Reesburgh was instructed to "tell the group that Grand thinks the group should get a good competition lawyer"?

A: Yes, I see that phrase.

Q: Do you remember who offered that suggestion to Mr. Reesburgh?

A: I did.

Q: OK, you did. Why did you do that?

A: Well, as I've said, I did have some bad feelings about any meetings or calls on this subject.

Q: Yes. But did your instruction to Mr. Reesburgh mean that you thought Grand could now join such meetings so long as the group got a good competition lawyer?

A: No, we weren't going to join the group or do anything but go to this meeting, that we thought was called by dealers, to show the flag.

Q: So if you weren't going to be joining the group, why did you care if the group hired a good competition attorney?

A: Well, yeah, I guess I used that phrase to impress upon Reese and Marc that this was serious and maybe even impress the others as well.

Q: Well, I can understand wanting your clients and fellow Grand employees to know what's going on—but why should you care if your competitors get into antitrust trouble?

A: Um, well, I guess I don't really care but I was concerned that CVMG would get caught up in such a suit or investigation and we were and are still members.

Q: Do you know if CVMG is part of this case?

A: My understanding is that they are co-defendants.

Q: Do you happen to know if CVMG or anybody else ever hired a good competition lawyer?

A: I don't think they ever did but I don't really know.

* * * * *

Q: OK, now after Mr. Reesburgh returned from the meeting, did any Grand employee attend any other meetings or calls involving your competitors and related to the topic of grey market vehicles?

35

A: To the best of my knowledge, no.

Q: Do you know if Frodo, Taylorita and Carizler representatives continued these meetings with either CVMG or CMVDA or both?

A: Yes, I think they did, well, I do know that there was some attempt to have such meetings—or more of them, I guess—because Lantesse asked if I would mind if he and CVMG continue to work them even though we were not participating.

Q: Is it normal for CVMG to do work on behalf of only some but not all its members?

A: No, not normal.

Q: Is it highly unusual?

A: Well, I don't know if I'd say "highly unusual" but it is the first time I can remember CVMG doing something like this if all its members weren't involved.

Q: Is that why Mr. Lantesse sought your permission to run these meetings?

A: Yes, I think so.

Q: And you said yes, you'd not object?

A: Correct, I would not object.

Q: Why did you say that?

A: Well, it looked like it was very important to some of my competitors, especially Jeff Lynch at Frodo, and so I thought it wouldn't do any harm if CVMG stayed involved. Also, I thought maybe it would mean that Jeff would say yes if I ever asked for similar treatment in the future.

Q: Did you ever get reports about what CVMG or CMVDA or the group of competitors was doing?

A: Yes, I think I got one email from Lantesse about one meeting—or maybe it was two meetings.

Q: As I hand you the next exhibit can you confirm that this is the one email you were referring to?

A. Yes, that's correct, and I see Lantesse refers to a couple meetings.

Q. Do you remember receiving this email from Lantesse?

A. No but I see I responded to it so I think I received it.

Q. Did you read it?

A. I don't remember but I'm not in the habit of responding to emails I haven't read so I probably did.

Q. You probably did read it?

A. Yes, that's what I said.

Q. So then you would have learned what CVMG and your competitors had been doing on the grey market issue?

A. Well, at some high level, I suppose.

Q. Did you ask for such summaries from Mr. Lantesse?

A. No, not at all.

Q. Did you tell him that you didn't want to receive any such summaries?

A. No, I don't think so.

Q. When you received this summary of those two meetings, did you tell him not to send any more?

A. No.

Q. Did you return the summary to him?

A. No.

Q. Did you delete it from your emails?

A. No, it looks like we found it so I could turn it over to you.

Q. Did you request any additional materials or information about the meetings?

A. No, as I said in the email response, "thanks, nothing more necessary."

Q. Does that mean that the email provided you all the information you needed?

A. Yes, I mean, no, I just meant, well I was just answering his question about whether I needed the full meeting minutes and I said I did not.

Q. So you took the time to email him that nothing more was necessary but you didn't tell him that you didn't want even these summaries, now or in the future?

A. I said what I said and I thought it got across the point that I didn't really want anything from him on these topics because Grand wasn't involved and we weren't going to get involved.

Q. Did you ever get any more summaries from Mr. Lantesse?

A. No.

Deposition of Peter J. Reesburgh
Offices of Gardner, Gervais and Patton
Toronto ON Canada

[excerpts]

* * *

PLAINTIFF COUNSEL Q: Mr. Reesburgh, prior to your meeting at the Fairmont Hotel in Toronto, did you have any other meetings or calls with Grand dealers or CMVDA representatives on grey market issues?

WITNESS A: Yes, just about every Grand dealer who got a chargeback called me to complain in some way.

Q: OK, but did you ever have any meetings on such topics with a group of Grand dealers?

A: Yes, Tim Roon of CMVDA arranged a meeting with three of our dealers and Marc Connote and me.

Q: And what was the purpose of that meeting?

A: So as I said, I'd heard all the complaints individually but the meeting was so that these three dealers could sort of represent all the others—and Tim definitely could represent all the dealers because that's his job—and we could have a discussion about Grand's policies regarding grey market vehicles.

Q: And did Mr. Roon and the dealers pass on the complaints of the Grand dealers?

A: Yes, although there was nothing I hadn't already heard and actually it wasn't as bad as I thought it was going to be.

Q: So do you think you sufficiently understood CMVDA's and your dealers' concerns on this subject?

A: Yes, probably did before the meeting and certainly did afterward.

Q: At this meeting, did the idea of an "industry solution" or Grand doing something with some of its competitors on the grey market issue come up?

A: No, I don't think so, it was all just focused on Grand—well, I think there were a couple mentions that Frodo's policies were worse but no suggestion that we ought to get together with them.

* * * * *

Q: Now I believe you testified earlier that you had a sufficient understanding of CMVDA's and your dealers' concerns relating to grey market from your Grand-only meeting and numerous phone calls from individual Grand dealers—is that right?

A: Yes.

Q: So what greater understanding did you hope to gain by attending this meeting at the Fairmont Hotel with CMVDA and representatives of your competitors?

A: So, it wasn't so much greater understanding of what the dealers were thinking as just making sure they couldn't later say that we didn't care about their concerns because we'd stiffed their organization when it was setting up the meeting.

Q: Did you hope to gain an understanding of how your competitors were approaching this same topic?

A: Not really, the Grand dealers who also held franchises of Frodo and the others gave us more than enough intelligence.

Q: Who invited you to this meeting?

A: Actually, Mike Lantesse invited Marc Connote to the meeting.

Q: Mike Lantesse of CVMG?

A: Correct.

Q: Not Tim Roon of CMVDA?

A: So Timmy called me and told me about it a couple days later, saying he'd asked Mike to invite all of us and he really hoped somebody from Grand would be attending because it was such an important issue to his constituents.

Q: Did CMVDA or CVMG set the agenda?

A: I don't know. Lantesse kicked off the meeting but Roon did a lot of the talking.

Q: How did you end up being the Grand representative at the meeting?

A: So we thought it was going to end up being a CMVDA, um, whine session, so Marc and Niall thought I should go because I'm the director of dealer relations.

Q: And your job is to listen to dealer whines?

A: Sometimes that seems like my only job.

* * * * *

Q: OK, when you got to the Fairmont, you found representatives of CVMG, Frodo, Taylorita and Carizler present but nobody from CMVDA, is that correct?

A: Yes, correct.

Q: Were you surprised?

A: Yes.

Q: Why?

A: So as I said, we thought it was sort of a chance for the dealers, through CMVDA, to air their complaints to all of us at once and so when they weren't there, I was a little taken aback.

Q: Why didn't you leave?

A: Well, Lantesse said Roon would be their shortly so I thought I could wait it out.

Q: And what happened while you waited it out?

A: So Jeff Lynch from Frodo talked a lot and suggested a few things that he thought the group should consider doing jointly.

Q: By the group, do you mean the manufacturers and the dealers or just the manufacturers?

A: So as I said, at this point it was just the manufacturers and CVMG so I don't think it included the dealers.

Q: Did you agree to any of the suggestions?

A: No, not at all. I just sort of sat and stewed because I thought it was a waste of time, I was only there to show the dealers that we cared for them and they weren't even there and then Lynch was going on and on with some ideas that I thought were, well, not something that were in Grand's best interests.

Q: Did you participate in the discussion?

A: For the most part no but then I couldn't take it any more and I said that I knew I couldn't agree on Grand's behalf to any of these schemes and that I was really there just to listen to Roon and then I blurted out that the group should probably get a good competition lawyer.

Q: Why did you make the suggestion about the competition lawyer?

A: So Niall had mentioned it at our meeting with Marc, I think sort of in jest, like these guys hadn't really thought these meetings all the way through and maybe they could use a little help. It came to mind because it seemed like a meeting that was supposed to be a listening session for dealer complaints had turned into a brainstorming session for manufacturers and so it seemed to me like the others really didn't know what they wanted to do, they just

39

wanted to be able to tell their American bosses that they were doing something. So I just kind of blurted it out, mostly in frustration.

Q: What was the reaction?

A: Actually, they kind of took it seriously, to my surprise because I think I was the only one in the room who wasn't a lawyer.

Q: Do you think the group really should have hired a good competition lawyer?

A: I don't know, that's Niall's job. Although maybe if they had, we all wouldn't be here right now, eh?

* * *

Q: Now Mr. Reesburgh, I want to ask just a couple questions about what actions GM or GMCL took regarding the grey market issues, OK?

A: Sure.

Q: OK, now during this timeframe, did GM or GMCL make any changes to what you have called your grey market policies?

A: Well, yes, it wasn't a huge change or really even a change at all but, yes, both GM and GMCL did clarify our policies during this timeframe.

Q: And what was that change—or, let's put it this way, what actions regarding grey market policies did GM and GMCL take during this timeframe?

A: We both did the same thing, about two weeks apart—I was busy and couldn't get the dealer bulletin out quite as quickly as my American counterparts. We told our dealers that effective with vehicle sales ninety days later, all vehicles would have to go to dealers in the right country for warranty work until the vehicles had accumulated 7500 miles or 12,500 km and were at least six months old.

Q: So let me see if I understand this action. If a vehicle was originally sold in Canada but, for whatever reason, was purchased by someone who was driving it in the U.S., that owner had to take the vehicle back to a Canadian GM dealer for warranty work until the vehicle was at least six months old and had 7500 miles—is that correct?

A: Yes, that's correct and vice versa is correct—if the car was American, it had to come back to the States for warranty work during that initial period.

Q: OK, and why did you tighten up the policy in this way.

A: Well, I'm not sure it really was a tightening of the written policy.

Q: Why? Well, let's start with, what was the prior written policy?

A: The car could only have its warranty work done in the right country for the entire life of the vehicle.

Q: Were there any exceptions to that policy, either in writing or in practice?

A: Well, yes, we did have a "tourist" or "snowbird" exception. That is, if the driver was just passing through the country—or, as is often true, somebody from Ontario spent a few months down in Florida—then a dealer in the country being visited could perform the warranty and be reimbursed.

Q: Was that the only exception to the prior written policy?

A: Yes, the only one in writing.

Q: Were there other exceptions in practice?

A: Well, if the customer complained loudly enough and we could determine that he or she was a good customer, we might OK it as well.

Q: Did those kind of exceptions happen a lot?

A: Well, I'm not sure what you mean by a lot but yes I think they were frequent.

Q: And so why did you want to change that policy?

A: Well, I, at least personally, didn't.

Q: OK, then who did?

A: The sales folks down in Detroit. They wanted to do something and show dealers that they'd done something. And I went along—well, I guess my friends in the States shared this rationale too—but I went along because I thought it would clarify the policy for dealers and customers.

Q: But it would clarify it by tightening it up over what the practice had been before the change, right?

A: Well, not necessarily, the old policy said you always had to go back to the right country for all warranty work for the term of the warranty and now it was just for 6 months and 12,500 km.

Q: Yes, that was the written policy but didn't you just say that the practice was to approve those warranty repairs despite that written policy?

A: No, not all the time.

Q: Are you aware of any times when, under the old policy, such warranty repairs for a vehicle that was in the "wrong" country were approved?

A: Oh yes, many times.

Q: And are you aware of any times when such repairs were disapproved—under the old policy.

A: Well, no.

Q: And now under the new policy, are there any exceptions in practice to the mileage/time requirements—has a vehicle warranty repair been approved even though the vehicle was in the "wrong" country and the vehicle was very new?

A: No, I know of no such exceptions.

Q: Do you know of any requests for such exceptions?

A: Well, the policy isn't that old but I know of two down in the States—but I'm really not the right person to ask on that, I wouldn't necessarily hear of all of them from down there but it's been silent here in Canada.

Q: Let's shift gears a little bit. When GM and GMCL made these changes—sorry, took these actions, these clarifications—do you know if all the other manufacturers were making changes at the same time?

A: All of them? No.

Q: Some of them?

A: Yes.

Q: Which one or ones?

A: Carizler had announced, probably six weeks earlier, that they were immediately changing their warranty—or maybe it was their warranty policy—such that the vehicles had to be taken back to the right country for all warranty repairs for the life of the warranty.

Q: So just like the GM and GM policy change or clarification except there was no grace period?

A: Yes, I guess that's about right but they announced it and implemented it right away and issued a press release with a lot of legal mumbo jumbo about the warranty being issued by a different Carizler subsidiary in the different countries and so, legally I guess, they felt they almost had to take this action.

Q: You think they took this action because their lawyers said they had to or because they wanted to reduce the incentive for someone to buy a grey market vehicle?

A: I don't know, you'll have to ask them.

Q: Thanks, we will. But you knew about this Carizler action while you were considering the action you ended up taking?

A: Yes, we all did on both sides of the border because it didn't seem to be well-received by dealers or in the press.

Q: And so you were worried about taking the same reputational hit?

A: Well, yes, we wanted to see how it would be accepted and then we could do our own thing—and that's one reason why we ended up doing what it is that we did.

Q: I see—and did you talk to anyone from Carizler about this warranty action it took?

A: No.

Q: Did you talk to anyone from Carizler about the action you were contemplating or ended up taking?

A: No.

Q: Did you consult CMVDA or CVMG before taking your action?

A: No, no need to, we thought it was the right action for us.

Deposition of Pierre Mallard
Offices of Gardner, Gervais and Patton
Toronto ON Canada

[excerpts]

* * * * *

PLAINTIFF COUNSEL Q: So Mr. Mallard, as Taylorita General Counsel and Director of Industry Relations, were you Taylorita's sole representative on the phone call arranged by CVMG and attended by Mr. Macdougall from Grand for only a few minutes?

WITNESS A: Yes, I was the sole Taylorita representative but I think you gave me a promotion when you mis-stated my title. I'm the GC and IR Director for Taylorita of Canada, not all of Taylorita.

Q: Yes, thank you for that correction. And were you the sole representative at the meeting that took place at the Fairmont Hotel in Toronto at which representatives of Frodo, Grand, Carizler, CMVDA and CVMG were present?

A: Correct, oui, I mean yes.

Q: Fine, and were you the sole representative for Taylorita at the subsequent meeting at which all the same entities except Grand were represented?

A: Yes.

Q: Thank you, merci. Now I'll break this down a little more later but for now, thinking about those three events together, is it your understanding that there was an agreement among the vehicle manufacturers to do something about grey market vehicles?

A: Yes, there certainly was an agreement that grey market vehicles were a problem for all of us, an industry problem really, and I think there was, I don't know about an agreement but really a consensus that we should do something together, or at least most of us, if we could.

DEFENSE COUNSEL Q: Can we go off the record for a moment?

[Discussion off the record]

PLAINTIFF COUNSEL Q: Mr. Mallard, did you want to add anything to your prior answer?

WITNESS A: Yes, I think I just to make clear what I said. There was never any agreement as such, just really an understanding by all of us that all of us faced the same problem and all of us, or at least most of us, thought it might be a good idea to at least consider if we could reach consensus on what could be done.

Q: Ok. Thanks for that clarification, that's good enough for me.

* * *

GRAND COUNSEL Q: Mr. Mallard, you testified earlier about the possibility of a consensus that all or most of the manufacturers thought it might be a good idea to consider what could be done about grey market vehicles—do you remember that?

A: Yes.

Q: OK, then, when you said "most of the manufacturers," were you excluding any manufacturers in particular?

A: Yes. Grand.

Q: You thought Grand had no interest in exploring the possibility of reaching such a consensus?

A: Correct, yes, I thought that was pretty clear.

Q: And why did you think it was pretty clear?

A: Well, first Niall joined that phone call for something like two minutes and made a speech about not wanting to do anything together and then hanging up. And then he didn't show up for the meeting at the Fairmont, he just sent Mr. Reesburgh who only seemed to want to listen, not talk, and then only listened to Mr. Roon from the dealers.

Q: So you thought Grand had no interest in even exploring the possibility of an agreement among manufacturers?

43

A: Yes, that came through very clearly.

Q: And do you think others, such as Mr. Lantesse, had the same opinion?

A: Oh yes, Mike was disappointed that Niall wouldn't join in because he thought it would be tough to get an industry solution that the dealers would like if Grand wasn't part of it so he said he'd keep working on Grand.

CHAPTER 3

VERTICAL ISSUES: PRICE AND NON-PRICE RESTRAINTS, TYING AND PRICE DISCRIMINATION

I. INTRODUCTION

This chapter covers a variety of antitrust issues that could arise in interactions between a seller and a buyer (usually a reseller). First, the seller and buyer could agree on restraints on the way that the product is priced or otherwise marketed to subsequent customers. Second, the seller might insist that the buyer purchase a second product in order to be able to purchase the first. Decades ago, all these kinds of restrictions were looked upon suspiciously by courts; now, all are judged under some form of the rule of reason standard and are likely to pass antitrust muster. Finally, the seller might sell the same product to one customer at a price lower than the price to a second customer. The chapter concludes with a discussion of the antitrust treatment of such price discrimination.

The simulation exercise in this chapter gives you the opportunity to: review select terms of a distribution agreement between a seller and a reselling buyer; consider whether any of those terms raise any of the many types of vertical issues discussed; communicate your conclusions to your client; and use the materials provided and the cases discussed herein to discuss resolution of allegations of vertical antitrust issues with counsel for the other party.

II. AN OVERVIEW OF THE LAW

Vertical issues arise between companies at different levels of the distribution chain (and, in an economist's drawing, that are connected by vertical lines). Any anticompetitive effects could be felt by either the buyer or the seller or the competitors of either. For many years, antitrust courts looked upon the vertical restraints discussed in this chapter with a great deal of suspicion. Some were even per se, that is, automatically, illegal. Academics and other antitrust thinkers convinced the courts that these restraints were often competitively benign or even beneficial to consumers. As a result, all of them are now judged under standards that make it much less likely that they will be found to be anticompetitive and, therefore, illegal.

One of the first types of vertical restraints to be judged under a more lenient standard was non-price vertical restraints. Such restraints restrict how resellers can market the products purchased from sellers. Examples include requirements that resellers sell from specified locations; use salespeople who have participated in certain kinds of training; and sell from stores or parts of stores that look a certain way. All these restraints had only an indirect effect on price. Such restraints were considered by the Supreme Court three times in the mid-20th Century, the final time in *Continental T.V. Inc. v. GTE Sylvania, Inc.*, 433 U.S. 36 (1977). In that case, the seller required its buyers to resell the televisions only within specified geographic territories. The Court found that such restraints should be judged under the rule of reason so any court could judge their net effect on competition. The Court described some of the potential procompetitive effects from such restraints, including inducing "competent and aggressive retailers to make the kind of investment of capital and labor that is often required in the distribution of [such] products." *Sylvania*, at 54. The main negative competitive effect from such restraints will be a loss of competition in the sale of that brand of television in the specified geographic area. That kind of competition—"intrabrand competition" to economists—is less important than competition among the various brands of televisions—that is, "interbrand competition." As the Court stated in a now famous quote, "Interbrand competition . . . is the primary concern of antitrust." *Sylvania*, at 51. The result is that all such restraints are now judged on their effect on interbrand competition under a rule of reason and usually found to be legal.

While the *Sylvania* Court decided that non-price vertical restraints were to be judged under the rule of reason, it maintained the rule that vertical price restraints were per se illegal. Therefore, the battle in many antitrust cases came down to whether the restraint was properly classified as a price or non-price restraint. Again, the antitrust academics went to work and explained that the categorization was unnecessary as the competitive effects of price and non-price restraints could be identical. For instance, when a retailer is forced to purchase a special display case for the products purchased from a seller, it is likely to raise its prices to recoup its extra costs. The Court began to accept that argument twenty years after *Sylvania* in *State Oil v. Khan*, 522 U.S. 3 (1997). There, a gasoline company had imposed a maximum resale price on its distributors. The Court overruled its earlier cases and decided that such maximum price vertical restraints were to be judged under the rule of reason. The Court thought that the incentives of the seller were aligned with the ultimate consumer. The rule of reason standard allowed for the consideration that the buyer might be the only reseller of the product ("Last Gas for 100 Miles," for instance) and the restraint would stop it from taking advantage of the situation and drastically increasing the price. When a seller can credibly claim such a rationale for the maximum price restraint, the restraint is likely to pass antitrust muster.

So after *State Oil*, the debate shifted to whether a price restraint was a maximum one to be judged under the rule of reason or one that set a minimum or the exact price, which were still per se illegal. This time, the Court took only ten years to modify the rules. In *Leegin Creative Leather Prods, Inc. v. PSKS*, 551 U.S. 877 (2007), it found that all vertical price restraints should be judged under the rule of reason. In that case, the seller of women's accessories had insisted that its resellers sell at or above certain prices so as to generate enough revenue to pay for the well-trained salespeople and comfortable showrooms it thought best displayed its products. The Court thought such price restraints could be competitively benign so long as there was no indication that they were mere covers for horizontal price agreements at the seller or reseller level. While there was a loss of price competition among resellers of that brand of accessories, those products still competed on price with other accessory brands—and, as the Court had said numerous times since *Sylvania*, interbrand competition is "the primary concern of antitrust." As a result, all price and non-price vertical restraints challenged under Sherman Act Section 1 are judged under the rule of reason. (Some state antitrust laws, such as those in California and New York, have been interpreted to go only as far as *State Oil* and not *Leegin*.)

A different vertical restraint that is treated more leniently now than in the past is tying. In this restraint, a buyer is forced to buy a second product that it might not want in order to purchase the first product that it really wants. For decades, courts struck down these arrangements as per se illegal, either because they offended some notion of personal liberty or because they were seen as a way of "leveraging" power in the first product to the market for the second product. The Court in *Jefferson Parish Hosp. Dist. No. 2 v. Hyde*, 466 U.S. 2 (1984) revisited the issue and explained when such arrangements would be considered anticompetitive. In that case, a local hospital required that patients purchase anesthesia services from one of its designated anesthesiologists in order to buy hospital services. While the Court issued multiple opinions, the case has been seen as establishing a test that condemned tying only if a buyer was forced to purchase two separate products and the seller had enough market power in the first product to actually "force" the purchase of the second product. Here, the Court found the hospital had only a 30% share of the market for hospital services. Because patients who wanted other anesthesia choices had a sufficient number of other hospital choices, the Court did not find the arrangement anticompetitive. While the Court clarified the standard to be used, it insisted on still calling it a "per se" test, although the analysis is much closer to a rule of reason.

Since then, courts, including the Supreme Court, have explored various aspects of the test, including when two products should be considered separate and the correct market definition to use when analyzing market power. In *Eastman Kodak Co. v. Image Technical Servs.*, 504 U.S. 451 (1992), the Court explored whether a company could have market power in the replacement parts for its durable products. Kodak had traditionally sold parts for its copiers to willing purchasers, including companies that competed with Kodak to service the copiers by installing the parts. It then changed its policy and sold parts only to buyers who also bought Kodak service or installed the parts themselves. Because Kodak was the only source of some of the parts, some independent service providers were harmed and sued. The Court found that Kodak was capable of having power in a market for replacement parts for Kodak copiers and, thus, could be guilty of anticompetitive tying. A vigorous dissent agreed with Kodak's argument that no matter what its share in any market for Kodak parts, its small share in the market for all copiers meant that it could not effectively wield any power in a Kodak parts market without fear of losing too many copier customers. As a result of the dissent, *Kodak* has been read to apply only when, as in the case, there are buyers who are "locked in" to a particular seller's brand and had no reason to suspect such a change in policy.

One final vertical issue is price discrimination. Congress has shown concern for a century for the fairness of one seller selling the same product to two different competing customers at two different prices. The result was the 1936 passage of the Robinson-Patman Act, 15 U.S.C. § 13, a complex amendment to the Clayton Act that has been the subject of much criticism. Unlike other antitrust laws, Robinson-Patman was almost certainly aimed at the protection of certain competitors (especially small grocery stores without the buying power of supermarkets) and not competition; yet it is part of the antitrust laws and one of its elements is "injury to competition." The result is a statute heavily criticized by academics and unenforced by government enforcers. Private litigants must prove several technical elements to skeptical courts to prevail on a claim. Yet, Robinson-Patman has resisted all attempts at repeal and still generates new private suits every year.

While Robinson-Patman has several prohibitions and some basic jurisdictional requirements, the elements of the standard price discrimination claim by a disadvantaged buyer can be easily summarized: such a plaintiff must show 1) a difference in price; 2) in contemporaneous sales from one seller to two buyers; 3) involving commodities, not services; 4) of like grade and quality; 5) that may injure competition. The statute also lists some defenses, including lower prices to meet competition or take account of lower costs of servicing certain customers. While the elements may be easy to summarize, decades of skepticism from courts have made them difficult to prove. A successful plaintiff must jump through several technical hoops.

The final element—injury to competition—is the one most often used by courts to ensure that Robinson-Patman is interpreted consistently with other antitrust laws. For decades, courts interpreted this element to allow one disadvantaged buyer to show that its injuries were sufficient to show injury to competition more generally. In *FTC v. Morton Salt*, 334 U.S. 37 (1948), the Supreme Court considered significant discounts to salt buyers who were willing to purchase very large quantities. While the Court admitted that the low prices were technically available to all purchasers, the huge quantities required meant they were not functionally available. As to proof of injury, the Court found a substantial price difference over a substantial period of time, even to just one buyer, was sufficient to raise a rebuttable presumption of injury to competition. This "*Morton Salt* presumption" eased the evidentiary burden on plaintiffs.

More recently, the Court and lower courts have often found evidence rebutting the presumption and breaking the causal chain between lower prices and lost sales. (They have also interpreted the other elements much more strictly.) One example is the Court's opinion in *Texaco Inc. v. Hasbrouck*, 496 U.S. 543 (1990). In that case, a gasoline company sold its product at a lower price to wholesalers who performed some distribution functions than it did to retailers who performed no such functions.

The Court recognized the theoretical possibility that reasonable "functional discounts" that took into account the cost or value of the function provided by the wholesaling buyer would not trigger the *Morton Salt* presumption. The Court found that the discounts in that case went beyond mere compensation for performing such functions and, therefore, could have injured both the disadvantaged buyer and competition.

A second example is the Court's opinion in *Volvo Trucks N.A. v. Reeder-Simco GMC*, 546 U.S. 164 (2006). In that case, a truck manufacturer offered varying discounts to its dealers, including the plaintiff, as each dealer bid against dealers of other manufacturers' trucks. The Court found the offered evidence insufficient to show competitive injury. In almost all the examples submitted, the plaintiff was not in competition with other dealers of the manufacturer for the same customer. Also, the plaintiff did not attempt to show that it regularly and systematically received lower discounts than other dealers of the manufacturer.

III. BACKGROUND

Meganami Corp. is the proud owner of the latest Japanese collectible craze getting ready to sweep across the U.S. and excite young and old collectors alike. Anna Mae is the name of the concept. In short, the concept tells the story of collectors—especially one young one named Huck—and their adventures as they try to collect all 149 "Ricks," magical creatures and each with special powers. The concept has been a wild success in Japan with a popular cartoon show and long lines in stores to buy the related trading card games and figurines embedded with special technology for future online variants.

Meganami U.S. Distribution Inc. expects to duplicate the Japanese success in the U.S. An English language version of the cartoon will be shown shortly in primetime on the popular Toon TV channel. The trading card game starter sets and booster packs and the figurines are ready to be shipped to the U.S. Some of Meganami's successful Japanese marketing elements are also being "imported" to the U.S. distribution network.

Specifically, the Anna Mae Distribution Agreement all prospective U.S. retailers must sign has some significant restrictions and requirements meant to mimic the successful Japanese marketing efforts. For instance, all retailers must buy from Meganami a large display case for nearly $1000 to properly showcase the card and figurine of all 149 Ricks at one time. Also, no trading card game starter set or booster pack or figurine can be sold to customers by retailers for a price higher than a price established by Meganami. These and other restrictions are meant to ensure that the Anna Mae products are sold in ways consistent with the Meganami corporate philosophy (and with its successful Japanese sales).

Meganami is targeting small, local toy and hobby shops for most of its distribution needs; however, it has also signed the distribution agreement with Fun iZ Us (FZU), one of the larger American toy retailers with locations across the country. Meganami has also taken two temporary steps to ensure appropriate inventory in stores at the launch of its products. First, it is offering a 10% discount for the next six months on all Ricks figurines purchased after the first 500 purchases. Second, to take care of a bottleneck in its manufacturing process, it is offering an additional 5% discount for the next six months when retailers are willing to accept the figurines in bulk and agree to place each one in its proper box.

One of those small, local toy and hobby shops who signed the distribution agreement is Taylor's Treasures and its owner, William Taylor. That company has one store each in Albany and Rochester NY. After signing the agreement and seeing the announcements of the two temporary discounts, Mr. Taylor has written a letter to Meganami officials complaining about several elements of this distribution system. First, he is upset that he must purchase such a large display case when he already has another one that, though smaller, seems perfectly adequate to him. Second, he understands that demand for Anna Mae products will be high at the launch; however, his years of experience with past crazes tell him that demand will cool off eventually. Before it does, he would like to set a resale price higher than that allowed by Meganami. Finally, he does not believe that he will be able to take complete advantage of either discount program; however, he fears that his only competition in upstate New York, FZU, will do so and Taylor will be at a disadvantage. Taylor has discussed these issues with his local Meganami sales representative and now has written the headquarters. He wants some changes made in the distribution plan or he will have his attorney contact Meganami.

Anna Mae to Rock U.S. Next Quarter

by Collections Illustrated Staff

Get ready for yet another collectible craze from Japan. "Anna Mae" has been a huge hit in Japan the last two months, with lines of kids—and adult collectors—lining up to buy the merchandise and then going home to watch the cartoons. Anna Mae owner Meganami plans to bring the craze to North America shortly. The trading card game and collectibles hit the U.S. next quarter, accompanied by an English language version of the show at a prime time on Toon TV.

The concept—and phenomenon—might sound familiar. The story is about a young boy named Huck who dreams of becoming a Master Collector of Ricks. Ricks are cute little creatures with different powers who battle with each other. Right now, there are 149 Ricks for Huck and his friends—and serious collectors like you—to catch. And of course, the first and most popular one is named Anna Mae.

There is a trading card game, with a starter set of forty cards, rules, dice and playmat. Booster packs contain seven cards each and include both Ricks and different cards to improve their powers. In addition, six to eight inch high figurines—"action figures" to the pre-teen boy market—of each Rick will be sold and include digital technology to interact with an online game under development and expected soon.

Meganami is signing up its U.S. distributors right now. Most of the early distributors are small, locally-owned hobby and collectible shops. It is widely expected that most of the distribution of both the trading card game and figurines will be done through such expert distributors who are willing and able to give the products the attention Meganami thinks they deserve. Early reports indicate that distributors will be required to display the products in special dedicated cases.

Meganami has confirmed that it also will distribute the products through one mass merchandiser, national toy chain Fun iZ Us (FZU). FZU confirmed last week that it has reached an agreement with Meganami to sell the products in many of its locations, as soon as each is equipped with the special display case.

The combination of local hobby shops and one national retailer is an unusual distribution scheme but, according to at least one expert, might be just right for Meganami. "They get the dedication of the local folks and the potential volume of FZU and all while everyone sells from the same display case—it just might work" said Roberta Lytle, noted toy collectible expert.

Pricing for the products has not been officially announced but our sources tell us the trading card game starter set is expected to retail for around $29.99 with additional packs of cards going for $3. The figurines are expected to retail for about $9.99. We are told that Meganami is pricing the products aggressively to successfully break into the competitive market for pre-teen boys and establish a base of fans for later online games. So far, the strategy is working well in Japan, with retailers sticking to the low prices and selling out their inventories quickly to hordes of crazed fans. We shall see if the same strategy translates to the U.S.

Anna Mae Distribution Agreement

[excerpts]

This AGREEMENT, effective as of _____ ("Effective Date") is entered into between MEGANAMI U.S. DISTRIBUTION INC., a Delaware corporation, on behalf of its parent, MEGANAMI CORP., a corporation organized under the laws of Japan (together "Meganami"), and _____ _____, an entity organized under the laws of _____ _____ ("Retailer").

RECITALS

WHEREAS Meganami has developed products related to its Anna Mae concept (as listed in Appendix B, which will be updated by Meganami from time to time)("Products") that it wishes to sell to consumers through various retailers, including Retailer;

WHEREAS Meganami intends to sell the Products to Retailer and wants Retailer to sell the Products to consumers in ways consistent with the Meganami corporate philosophy of fair dealing and close attention to a customer's needs;

WHEREAS Meganami believes that when it and retailers, including Retailer, maintain consistency with that philosophy that consumers will be pleased with their purchases of the Products and Meganami and Retailer will be successful in all senses; and

WHEREAS this Agreement sets out the ways in which that corporate philosophy is to be translated to distribution of the Products.

THEREFORE, the Parties agree as follows:

1. RETAILER AS NON-EXCLUSIVE RETAILER OF PRODUCTS. Meganami agrees to sell Products and Retailer agrees to purchase and resell Products under the terms of this Agreement. Retailer acknowledges that Meganami may appoint other retailers of Products that will purchase and resell Products under these or substantially similar terms.

* * *

5. RETAILER TO SELL PRODUCTS CONSISTENT WITH MEGANAMI CORPORATE PHILOSOPHY. Retailer agrees to sell the Products in a way consistent with the Meganami corporate philosophy detailed in the Recitals above, including but not limited to complying with the terms of this Section.

A. QUANTITIES. Retailer agrees to purchase and resell Products in quantities consistent with the Meganami corporate philosophy.

B. SALES TO END USERS. Retailer agrees to take all reasonable steps to sell the Products only to those customers who will not resell the Products without first using them or holding them for long-term investment. Should Meganami discover a Product sold by Retailer that has been resold by a customer in a way that, in Meganami's reasonable interpretation, is not in conformance with this provision, Meganami may take all reasonable steps to recover the damages to its reputation and prevent a recurrence of the breach, up to and including termination of this agreement.

C. DISPLAY OF PRODUCTS TO END USERS. Retailer agrees to display all Products for resale in a way consistent with the then current Rules for Resale of Products ("Resale Rules"). The current Resale Rules are contained in Appendix A to this Agreement and may be updated by Meganami from time to time. To ensure a consistently high level of display that is consistent with Meganami's corporate philosophy, Retailer will purchase from Meganami or its designate any special display cases or shelving required by the Resale Rules. Retailer also agrees to have available a staff of properly-trained sales personnel adequate to meet the reasonable expectations of Product customers.

Retailer acknowledges that this Agreement does not constitute a franchise agreement under the laws of any jurisdiction. Retailer further acknowledges that it may use its best judgment, consistent with this Agreement and the Meganami corporate philosophy, to develop and implement marketing and sales plans. Finally, Retailer acknowledges that the cost to Retailer of any special display cases or shelving purchased from Meganami or its designate under the Resale Rules is fair compensation for those items and no portion of that cost shall be considered a franchise fee.

D. RESALE PRICES OF PRODUCTS. Retailer acknowledges and agrees with Meganami that sale of a Product to consumers at too high a price or at a price different than the price offered to other consumers is not consistent with the Meganami corporate philosophy. Therefore, Retailer agrees to resell the Products at a price of its own choosing but no higher than the then-current suggested retail price provided by Meganami in the Resale Rules. Retailer agrees to offer that same price to all consumers making reasonably contemporaneous purchases.

Meganami agrees that sales of Products by Retailer at prices lower than Meganami's then-current suggested retail price is consistent with Meganami's corporate philosophy. Retailer acknowledges that the price at which it chooses to resell the Products may be lower than the then-current suggested retail price provided by Meganami.

* * *

17. TERM AND TERMINATION. Unless otherwise terminated or extended through a method consistent with this Agreement, this Agreement shall expire at the end of the 24th full month following the effective date of this Agreement. Either Party may terminate the agreement for any or no reason with ninety day written notice to the other Party. Meganami may terminate the agreement in the case of a substantial breach by Retailer after thirty day written notice to Retailer.

* * *

Appendix A

Rules for Resale of Products

Retailer agrees to sell the Products in a way consistent with the Meganami corporate philosophy, including but not limited to complying with these Resale Rules.

DISPLAY CASE. Meganami has determined that it is important for the Products to be displayed and sold in a manner consistent from retailer to retailer. Also, that display must effectively display all the Ricks at one time in an appealing way and in the order consistent with the Anna Mae story told in various media. In that way, the Retailer will be paying close attention to the Anna Mae customer's needs.

Therefore, Meganami has determined that Retailer must purchase one Display Case X43561 ("Display Case") from Meganami for each of Retailer's sales locations. The Display Case has appropriate locations and signage for each of the current Ricks figurines and other Products. The Display Case is six feet wide by six feet high by two feet deep and is delivered fully assembled and with instructions for proper display of the Products. Retailer will receive the Display Case before or at the same time as Retailer's initial shipment of Products. Retailer is to set up the Display Case in a prominent place in its retail location and properly display the Products before any retail sales. Retailer will be invoiced for the $995 cost of the Display Case and payment terms for the Display Case will be consistent with those applicable to the Products.

SUGGESTED RESALE PRICES. Meganami believes in fair dealing for its customers. As a result, it prices its Products to customers such as Retailer at prices that allow for a fair return on investment for both Parties. It also believes that Retailer and other retailers should price the Products to the final customer at a price that is low enough to allow many customers to enjoy the Products but high enough to allow Retailer to earn a fair return on its investment in the marketing of the Products. Meganami also believes that customers should and do expect to be charged a fair price that is identical to the price paid by other customers purchasing the Product reasonably contemporaneously.

Therefore, Meganami has determined that Retailer must choose its own prices to its customers and those prices should be the same for all customers purchasing the Products reasonably contemporaneously. Also, Retailer's prices should be no higher than the Meganami Suggested Resale Prices listed as part of these Resale Rules or as subsequently notified. Retailer remains free to sell any Product at a price lower than the Suggested Resale Prices.

Suggested Resale Prices (before applicable taxes)

Anna Mae Starter Set: $29.99

Anna Mae Booster Packs: $3

Anna Mae Ricks Figurines: $9.99

RESALE RULE CHANGES. Meganami will communicate to Retailer any changes or additions to these Resale Rules and give adequate notice before any implementation. Meganami's corporate philosophy will not change.

Anna Mae Price Discount Announcement

To: Anna Mae Retailers

Fm: Anna Mae Sales Team

Your Anna Mae Sales Team is extremely excited as we begin distribution of our trading card games, booster packs and figurines around the U.S. We hope all of you are too—and from the reactions we've seen from those of you already displaying the products, we think all of you are. To keep that excitement growing, we came up with two new programs that we think you'll love.

First, we want to make sure that all of you have a great and broad supply of Ricks figurines ready to sell at all times. Our customers in Japan just love seeing all 149 Ricks in the display case. To keep all 149 slots occupied (with back ups ready to go), we have a special program open for the next six months. After you order your first 500 Ricks, every subsequent one you order during the next six months will be sold to you at a 10% discount. Nothing you need to do to register for this program—our ordering system will keep track and automatically take the discount off the price of your Ricks order 501 and beyond for the next six months from today. While which Ricks you order is completely your choice, you can talk to your Anna Mae sales representative for information on which characters are most popular in Japan and other parts of the U.S. Don't delay, order now to make sure your sales launch is fantastic!

Also, our colleagues in distribution tell us that they have some temporary issues in taking the figurines at the end of the manufacturing process and marrying them up with the box and printed material that goes in the box. We have a new system that solves the issue but will take a few months to implement. Because we don't want you to have any delay in getting all the Ricks you want in your display case, we are now extending you another special offer for the next six months. If you are willing, we will send you figurines packed in bulk and, separately, the correct boxes and printed material and you can marry up all of it. The bulk figurines need not be the same Rick. Those retailers who take advantage of this offer will have an additional 5% off the cost of each Rick. If you want to participate, you can choose to do so on some or all of your orders—just talk to your sales representative and he or she will provide you all the details.

And yes, you can combine both these offers—and we hope you do!

Any questions, please be sure to contact your local sales representative—and Happy Selling!

Taylor's Treasures

Delighting Customers in Albany and Rochester

Since 1983

Meganami U.S. Distribution Corporation

1875 Century Park East

Suite 1040

Los Angeles CA 90067

Dear Sir/Madam:

I am the owner of Taylor's Treasures, the best and most successful hobby and collectibles store in upstate New York. I write to express my displeasure with some of the terms of the Anna Mae distribution agreement I recently signed.

First, I object to having to pay you about $1000 for a display case that I don't really need. Your case would be the biggest one I have ever had in either location and will overwhelm my store. I have an excellent case from our days selling Digimon figurines that fits in my store much better and would display 20 Ricks at a time. I would agree to rotate the Ricks displayed every other day. I object to being forced to buy a case that I don't really need to get the figurines and trading card games that I can only get from you. Also, I think my proposal will sell more Ricks as my clientele will be excited to see different Ricks every few days. I suggested this approach to my Meganami representative, Tony Boles, and he told me to take it to you.

Second, I object to your maximum resale prices. This is America and I should be allowed to set the sale prices on products that are mine now because I purchased them from you. I don't plan to gouge my customers because they and I know that they won't come back if I don't treat them well. But they also understand that I have to make money while I can so I can keep serving them. Your corporate philosophy talks about treating customers well— remember, I'm your first customer. Again, Tony said to take it up with you.

Finally, I object to your volume discounts that you are offering both me and my only competitors in upstate New York, Fun iZ Us. While I could—and expect to—buy and resell 500 figurines in the next 6 months, I can't buy them all right away like I'm sure FZU can. I just don't have the storage space they have. That means they'll have a cost advantage over me and that's not fair. Also, I don't have the personnel to take advantage of the program of buying the figurines in bulk and boxing them myself—I thought that's what I was paying you to do. Again, I'll bet FZU can and does take advantage of that program.

Tony has been a great sales rep but these issues are ones with headquarters. Please contact me in the next week to discuss these issues. If not, my attorney will contact you.

Sincerely

William Taylor

Taylor's Treasures HQ
501 New Karner Rd
Albany NY 12205
(518) 869-9000

CHAPTER 4

MONOPOLIZATION THROUGH DISCOUNTS

I. INTRODUCTION

The law of monopolization is the most controversial area of antitrust law. Other areas can generate debates over application of a specific set of facts but most antitrust practitioners agree on the law. Not so with monopolization. At most, antitrust courts and lawyers agree on a two-part test before finding a violation of Sherman Act Section 2: First, the defendant must be a "monopolist," usually defined as having a high market share and the ability to raise prices; and second, the monopolist must be "monopolizing," that is, taking inappropriate steps to maintain that monopoly. It is the second part of the test that creates the most controversy because courts do not want to condemn hard competition that is good for consumers.

There is no single test for "monopolization"; instead, courts and theorists have developed several tests depending on the actions being taken by a monopolist. Often those actions include various types of price discounts. The tests developed to judge discounts attempt to balance the obvious benefits to customers with the potential for shutting out a monopolist's rival from important sales. This chapter reviews the tests used by courts to determine if such discounts amount to monopolization. Chapter 5 reviews the tests used to determine when a monopolist must deal with a rival.

The simulation exercise in this chapter gives you an opportunity to: review the terms of a loyalty discount pricing program introduced by a company that might be considered a monopolist; review written complaints about the program from a supplier and a customer; review internal documents regarding the rationale for the program; and use these materials provided and the cases discussed herein to practice explaining difficult antitrust topics to in-house counsel.

II. AN OVERVIEW OF THE LAW

Sherman Act Section 2 is the attempt by the antitrust laws to prevent unilateral action that causes harm to competition. Literally, the statute makes a felon of "every person who shall monopolize, or attempt to monopolize . . . any part of the trade or commerce among the several States, or with foreign nations." The key term is "monopolize," a verb, instead of "monopolist," a noun. Only monopolists who monopolize violate Section 2. As the Supreme Court has said, the offense "has two elements: (1) the possession of monopoly power in the relevant market and (2) the willful acquisition or maintenance of that power, as distinguished from growth or development as a consequence of a superior product, business acumen or historic accident." *U.S. v. Grinnell Corp.*, 384 U.S. 563, 570–571 (1966). Other jurisdictions around the globe apply similar two part tests to their unilateral conduct statutes.

The first element, often described as "monopoly power," can be difficult to prove in any particular matter but, theoretically, is the element where there is widespread agreement. In most cases, the proof consists of a high market share in a relevant market plus evidence of the ability to price without regard to the price set by any competitors. Determining market shares, of course, requires the determination of the relevant product and geographic markets. Fortunately, antitrust courts and enforcers have developed robust methods for defining product markets. The Supreme Court expressed a rough version of the test decades ago in "the Cellophane case" when it described the search for all substitute products as follows: [whether products are substitutes and therefore in the same market] "depends on how different from one another are the offered commodities in character or use, [and] how far buyers will go to substitute on commodity for another . . . [and whether they are] reasonably interchangeable by consumers for the same purpose." *U.S. v. E.I. duPont de Nemours & Co.*, 351 U.S. 377, 393 (1956). Since the opinion in the Cellophane case, antitrust enforcers have developed a more precise process for product and geographic market definition in merger reviews, although the process is used for other antitrust purposes as well. That process has been updated and published several times in the *Horizontal Merger Guidelines* published by the Federal Trade Commission and Department of Justice Antitrust Division. Under the *Guidelines*, enforcers or a court should begin with the narrowest definition of a product market and assume a monopolist. Then, the monopolist is assumed to impose a "small but significant non-transitory increase in price" and the reaction of consumers is estimated. If enough consumers would start buying a different product such that the price increase would not be profitable for the hypothetical monopolist, that other product is added to the market definition and the process is repeated. The same iterative process is used to determine the relevant geographic market as well.

Once the market is determined, historical sales data or expert estimates are used to derive the market share of the alleged "monopolist." While a market share of one hundred percent is not necessary to show monopoly power, courts have not set a specific lower threshold. The Supreme Court has said that a 75% share would have constituted a monopoly in *U.S. v. E.I. duPont de Nemours & Co.*, 351 U.S. 377, 391 (1956). Lower courts have rarely found monopoly power with a share lower than 50%. Even in cases with shares above 50%, determination of a high market share usually is not the end of the analysis; instead, courts then search for other evidence to confirm that the defendant has some ability to raise prices without fear of rival retaliation. A finding of monopoly power is more likely when the few remaining competitors are unlikely to expand output and potential competitors are unlikely to overcome barriers to entry in response to a price increase by a monopolist.

The second element of a Section 2 claim—monopolization—has been much more controversial both in theory and in application to any particular set of facts. The requirement even has several names: monopolization, exclusionary conduct, anticompetitive conduct, monopoly maintenance. Courts, academics, commissions and enforcers have spent years trying to develop an overall description that would prevent such "monopolization" without stopping tough competitive behavior beneficial to consumers. Those efforts have been unsuccessful. Therefore, courts instead have used a category approach, developing tests for different categories of conduct to determine when it rises to "monopolization." For conduct involving price discounts, the two main tests are the price/cost test and the foreclosure test.

The price/cost test was developed to judge allegations of "predatory pricing." Under that theory, a competitor sets very low, usually unprofitable, prices in hopes of driving out current competitors and then raising its prices to a much higher level. The Supreme Court confronted that theory and developed the price/cost test in *Brooke Group Ltd. v. Brown & Williamson Tobacco Co.*, 509 U.S. 209 (1993). There, one cigarette manufacturer claimed that a rival priced its generic cigarettes very low in order to convince the first manufacturer to leave the market or raise its prices. The Court did not want to chill the low prices that benefit consumers except in the most extreme cases; therefore, it set out a two part test that is very difficult for any plaintiffs alleging such conduct to meet. First, the plaintiff must prove "that the prices complained of are below an appropriate measure of its rival's costs." *Brooke Group*, at 224. While not fully explained by the Court, the concept of "appropriate measure of . . . costs" has come to mean a price not just at a loss but price below the company's average variable costs. The rationale for this prong is that a competitor selling one more product at a price lower than the cost of producing that marginal product would only do so to harm its rivals. Second, the plaintiff must prove that its low-pricing rival has "a dangerous probability of recouping its investment in below cost prices." *Brooke Group*, at 224. Recoupment means that after the plaintiff is driven out of the market, the defendant has the ability to keep the plaintiff—and all other current or potential rivals—out of the market so it can raise prices well above its costs to recover its losses and more. The Court in *Brooke Group* found that recoupment was not sustainable on the record before it.

The price/cost or *Brooke Group* test has been used by courts in subsequent cases alleging monopolization through pricing actions. The Supreme Court itself modified the test to apply to an allegation that an alleged monopsonist—someone with very strong buying, not selling, power—paid a predatorily high price for inputs in order to drive its rivals from the market. *Weyerhaeuser Co. v. Ross-Simmons Hardwood Lumber Co., Inc.*, 549 U.S. 312 (2007).

The second main test to determine if discounts by a monopolist violate Section 2—the foreclosure test—is derived from exclusive dealing cases. In those cases, a buyer agrees to buy a particular product only from one seller. (The same analysis would apply if a seller agreed to sell only to one buyer.) The parties and their ultimate customers benefit from reduced costs from greater certainty in their supply and demand of the product. Other sellers, however, are "foreclosed" from selling the product to the buyer. As the Supreme Court described in *Tampa Electric v. Nashville Coal*, 365 U.S. 320 (1961), that foreclosure has a negative effect on competition that outweighs any benefits only in unusual circumstances, such as where the buyer purchases a large percentage of the product sold. In *Tampa Electric*, the Court found no substantial foreclosure when a utility agreed to buy its coal needs for twenty years from one supplier because, while the quantities to be purchased were absolutely huge, they made up only a small percentage of the properly-defined market. Other cases have considered aspects of the buyer besides its quantity of purchases, including whether it is a special retailer, foreclosure from which would harm competition among its suppliers.

Some courts have adopted this foreclosure analysis to judge whether a monopolist's discount pricing practices, such as loyalty discounts and bundling, amount to anticompetitive behavior. In loyalty discount cases, buyers receive discounts if they purchase some large percentage (but less than 100%) of their needs from one buyer over a specified period of time. Buyers benefit from the lower prices while suppliers can increase their sales. If enough buyers participate in the program, however, competitors of the seller might be foreclosed from a substantial portion of the market. If the loyalty discounts are deep enough, buyers might think it necessary to accept them to remain competitive with their rivals, even if they would prefer to deal with a more diverse set of suppliers. Again, the result could be foreclosure of other sellers and long-term loss of competition.

While the Supreme Court has not wrestled with these questions for decades, several appellate courts have considered the circumstances under which such loyalty discounts could be considered "monopolization." In *Concord Boat v. Brunswick Corp.*, 207 F.3d 1039 (8th Cir. 2000), the Eighth Circuit found that the loyalty discount program offered by monopolist marine engine builder Brunswick did not foreclose other actual or potential engine suppliers. Brunswick's program offered 1–3% discounts if boat builders like the plaintiffs purchased 60–80% of their engine needs from Brunswick. The court found that engine competitors were not foreclosed even from the sales Brunswick made because the discount program did not require a long-term agreement and boat builders were free to switch to other suppliers—and many did. Also, the court found no significant barriers to entry facing potential engine suppliers. While the court focused on the foreclosure analysis, it did also cover the price/cost test by noting that the plaintiffs did not argue that Brunswick's discounts drove its net prices below any measure of its cost.

The Third Circuit confronted the choice between the price/cost test and foreclosure analysis in *ZF Meritor LLC v. Eaton Corp.*, 696 F.3d 254 (3rd Cir. 2012). Eaton was the dominant manufacturer of manual transmissions for large trucks. ZF Meritor was a joint venture of a small current competitor and potential competitor that also sold those transmissions. In response to ZF Meritor's formation, Eaton offered all the truck builders above-cost discounts if they agreed to purchase 65–95% of their transmission needs for several years and take certain steps to market Eaton's transmissions more prominently. All the truck builders agreed and ZF Meritor ended up exiting the market and suing. A majority of the court rejected Eaton's argument that it must apply *Brooke Group* and find the program presumptively legal. The court said that test applied only when price was the predominant mechanism of exclusion. Here, the court found non-price elements of the program as well, such as the marketing requirements. It also found substantial foreclosure because the buyers felt obligated to agree to these long contracts because of fear that Eaton would stop supplying any transmissions absent the agreement. The dissent would have used passing the *Brooke Group* test as a rebuttable presumption of legality for any discount program and saw insufficient evidence to overcome that presumption.

The Third Circuit again analyzed the potential competitive effects of loyalty pricing in *Eisai, Inc. v. Sanofi Aventis U.S., LLC*, 821 F.3d 394 (3rd Cir. 2016). A much smaller producer of a drug claimed that the dominant producer of drugs for particular ailments used volume and share discounts to foreclose sales to hospitals and other large buyers. The court found significant two distinctions from the discount program in *ZF Meritor*: First, hospitals that took the defendant's discounts were not precluded from also purchasing and "marketing" the plaintiff's drugs and, second, the defendant never threatened to stop supplying hospitals that chose not to qualify for a discount. The court explained that foreclosure was not when many customers chose the defendant's product but when "the defendant's anticompetitive conduct rendered that choice meaningless." Because so few customers were denied a meaningful choice by the defendant's discount program, the court found no substantial foreclosure.

Appellate courts have also struggled with the proper test to apply when a seller offers a discount only when a buyer purchases a bundle of products. In *LePage's Inc. v. 3M*, 324 F.3d 141 (3rd Cir. 2003) (en banc), 3M offered rebates to buyers like Wal-Mart if it purchased large or increasing quantities of 3M products across many product lines. LePage's claimed it was foreclosed and could not effectively compete because it only sold one product, transparent tape. This court also rejected application of the price/cost test of *Brooke Group* because LePage's claim was not strictly predatory pricing. Instead, the court applied a variation of the foreclosure analysis and found that 3M monopolized the transparent tape market by effectively foreclosing a single product rival from achieving economies of scale with key distribution channels. In *Cascade Health Solutions v. PeaceHealth*, 502 F.3d 895 (9th Cir. 2007), the Ninth Circuit faced a similar set of facts: One hospital system offered discounts to buyers who agreed to buy primary, secondary and tertiary care from it. A system that offered only primary and secondary care sued. The court applied a version of the price/cost test that would attribute the discount on the entire bundle to just those competitive products and then compare it to the defendant's average variable costs.

III. BACKGROUND

The Anniston Transmission Division of Grand Motors has instituted a loyalty pricing program. Anniston is the leading supplier of automatic transmissions for medium and heavy duty trucks. Its main competitor is a German company, ZX, that recently tried to acquire Anniston from Grand. That transaction was abandoned when the Department of Justice Antitrust Division objected to it and described Anniston as a "monopolist" in markets for sales of automatic transmissions for trucks to be used in certain stop-and-go vocations such as school buses and garbage trucks. Now once again part of Grand, Anniston hopes to use this loyalty pricing program to jumpstart sales and convince more truck builders and truck buyers to use automatics instead of manual transmissions.

The details of the program were sent to Anniston's direct customers, the truck builders, without any legal review. The following details quickly became well-known within the industry. Truck builders can qualify for a 20% discount on all Anniston Automatics they purchase over the next twelve months by completing a short registration form. On the form, the truck builders list all the vocations in which their trucks are sold and used. For each and every vocation, the truck builders commit to selling 50% of their trucks with an automatic transmission. Ninety percent of those automatic transmissions must be Anniston Automatics.

The Anniston sales and marketing leaders understood that the reaction to the loyalty pricing program—dubbed the "Anniston Advantage"—would be varied. For some vocations like school buses, the 50% threshold would be easy to meet. For others, like line-haul trucks, it would require a significant increase in automatic penetration. So companies that sell trucks only to vocations that already use plenty of automatics would have no problems meeting that target; those truck builders that sell in several vocations would need to significantly increase the number of automatics purchases to qualify for the discounts. Those same Anniston leaders realized that the 20% discount is significant and would be highly enticing to customers. Yet the program excluded certain transmissions used only in military vocations and all sales of replacement parts and, therefore, the Anniston financial staff has determined that Anniston would remain profitable during the one year term of the program.

The expectation that industry reaction would be varied turned out to be correct. Some truck builders responded favorably and indicated that they would register. One truck builder, Freeleaner, however, had its General Counsel write her Anniston counterpart and threaten a monopolization lawsuit. As a large customer of Anniston, Freeleaner has spent enough time investigating Anniston's facilities and costs and believes that sales at a 20% discount must be at a significant loss. It fears that there is a real chance that ZX will stop selling automatic transmissions in the U.S. Also, Freeleaner sells trucks in a wide variety of vocations. For those vocations that already have a high automatic penetration, Freeleaner feels forced to join the program in order to stay competitive with its competitors who only sell into those vocations. Yet, Freeleaner must also purchase a significantly increased number of automatic transmissions for other vocations and, almost certainly, drastically discount the price of the truck to incentivize truck buyers to purchase them. The result will be both financial and reputational losses for Freeleaner, affecting their ability to invest in future innovation. Finally, Freeleaner believes that the 90% threshold for Anniston Automatics will leave so few sales open to ZX that they likely will leave the market.

The Anniston General Counsel also received a note from his ZX counterpart. The two of them had grown close during the failed acquisition and the ZX attorney learned a great deal about Anniston. The ZX attorney has written a short note making no overt threats but raising the possibility that the Anniston Automatics would be sold at a loss under the program. He also thinks the 90% threshold will foreclose a significant portion of the markets to ZX and, as a result, ZX's sales will suffer.

To: Valued Anniston Transmission Original Equipment Customer

Fm: John Hattley, Anniston Director of Sales

Re: Exciting New Opportunity—The Anniston Advantage Program

I'm excited to announce a new program to help you introduce the advantages of Anniston automatic transmissions to even more of your customers—the Anniston Advantage Program. We think this program will help you take your truck sales to the next level while helping your customers get to the next level of driving safety, fuel efficiency and comfort.

Here's how the Anniston Advantage Program works: First, you and your Anniston sales representative register you in the program and ensure we know all the vocations in which you sell your medium and heavy duty trucks in the U.S. Then you commit to selling at least 50% of your trucks in each of the vocations you service with an automatic transmission. And for those automatics, you commit that at least 90% of those automatics will be Anniston Automatics, recognized for decades as the leader in automatics. Once you've made those commitments, Anniston will take 20% off the price of each and every Anniston Automatic you buy for the next twelve months.

That's money that stays in your pocket and that you can use as you please—passing on to the end user, demonstrating the many benefits of Anniston Automatics—you make the choice. And we know you can help your customers make the right choice—an Anniston Automatic.

Your Anniston sales representative will have all the other details you'll need to understand the program—make sure you take a close look and talk with your representative. I'm also available to answer any questions. Sign up for this program will be for a limited time. Make sure you get the advantages of the Anniston Advantage Program to help your customers get all the advantages of Anniston Automatics.

Happy Selling!

Leaning Forward

General Counsel, 600 W. Main Street, LaGrange IL

Jack Jacobson, Esq
General Counsel
Anniston Transmission Division
Grand Motors Corporation
1212 Speedway Avenue
Mail Stop 37333
Westerville, OH

Dear Mr. Jacobson:

Re: **Anniston Advantage Program**

As you will recall from our previous correspondence on the purchase order terms and conditions last year, I am the Freeleaner General Counsel. I write today because of our extreme concern that the Anniston Advantage Program is harmful to Freeleaner and violates both federal and state antitrust laws. If Anniston does not immediately rescind the program, you will leave us no other choice but to file suit and seek both injunctive and compensatory relief.

We do not make such accusations against a supplier lightly. We base our conclusion on the description of the program from Mr. Hattley; the further material and answers to our questions received from your sales representative, Mr. Burson; and an extensive discussion I personally had with Mona Gans, former FTC Chair and current head of the antitrust practice at Kurnlap & Wallace. I prepared the following points with the assistance of Ms. Gans.

First, it appears to us that the discounts being offered must mean Anniston will be selling these products at a loss. While our supplier audit was several months ago, it seems unlikely that Anniston's margins have changed considerably in the meantime. If our assumptions are correct, then our position is supported by both the *Concord Boat* case in the 8th Circuit and the *LePage's* and *Eisai* cases in the 3rd.

While predatory pricing schemes "are rarely tried and even more rarely successful," recent scholarship shows the possibility of success with such schemes in markets where share is high and other markets provide means to fund such a scheme. As you and the rest of us learned during the recent investigation of your proposed ZX transaction, Anniston can be said to be a monopolist in certain markets for automatic transmissions for certain vocations. Also, Mr. Burson confirmed for us that your sales to the military and your part sales are not affected by the Advantage program. We think that combination makes it more likely that a court would find it possible that Anniston has market power and is taking inappropriate acts to protect it.

It might seem odd for a customer to describe a discount program as anticompetitive; however, we think this program will end up harming us in the near future and immediately. First, we see very little real choice but to take the program and try to convince our customers to make it work. As you well know, customers in the transit bus and garbage truck vocations insist on an automatic transmission. The margins in the prices of trucks that meet those vocations' needs are slim. A couple hundred dollars on the cost of the automatic transmission can mean the difference between winning and losing the bid. So we feel like we have no choice but to participate in the program so we are not at a significant disadvantage to our competitors, many of whom make trucks that only use automatic transmissions. We strongly suspect all manufacturers of transit buses and garbage trucks, at least, would agree. If so, ZX could be foreclosed from many of the key automatic transmission vocations and eventually have to pull out of the U.S., leaving us with one fewer key supplier.

Our damages would also occur immediately. The requirement to purchase automatic transmissions for 50% of our sales in each of our vocations means that we will need to build many more Freeleaner trucks with automatics than customers in some vocations really want. Because customers in those vocations are very price-sensitive, we will need to severely discount our trucks. Those discounts are sure to damage Freeleaner's product reputation and exceed the discounts received on the Anniston transmissions, meaning we will need to pay much more and in various ways to obtain a discount from you. Also, we fear that the sales loss suffered by manual producers, even Eden Transmissions, will eventually affect us in the form of lower product investment and higher prices.

We understand Anniston's interest in pushing for greater automatic penetration and trying to grab the few automatic sales you do not already have. We think the Advantage Program, however, pushes the end user further than he or she wants to go and in a way that squeezes out your main competitor and damages direct customers like Freeleaner.

Please contact me within a week to tell me how you will withdraw the program from the marketplace. If I do not hear from you by then, K&W has standing instructions from me to file suit.

Sincerely,

Linda Thompson
General Counsel
Freeleaner Trucking Corporation

[ZX Email]

To: Jack Jacobson, General Counsel Anniston Transmission

From: Helmut Goher, General Counsel ZX Corporation

Jack—Good to email you again, although not under the circumstances I would have liked. I'm still sorry that we couldn't complete the transaction but life does indeed go on.

One of my sales guys gave me some interesting news last night. He said that you guys had started some sort of new sales program, called something like Anniston Advantage. Based on the description—and none of us here have seen any customer bulletins or can claim to know all the facts—it raises some issues for me.

As we understand it, customers are being offered something like a 20% discount if they buy enough automatics for some or all of their vocations and if 90% of those automatics are Annistons. I don't want you to confirm the actual discount for me—that's up for you to decide—but based on what I remember, that discount seems to me like one at which you'll be losing money.

Also, the 90% figure, if true and if every customer opts in, will really put a crimp in ZX's plans. We could be foreclosed from enough potential sales that we could suffer.

The program just seems risky and inconsistent with the approach we discussed as we were doing due diligence with you guys. I fear it might be another time that Johnny H got out ahead of his blocking (if I'm correctly using the American football term). Anyway, I thought I'd bring it to your attention. If you're comfortable with it, that's all I need to know right now—although my sales folks might take a little convincing.

Hope to hear from you soon—thanks.

[Anniston Email]

To: Jack Jacobson, Anniston General Counsel

From: John Hattley, Anniston Director of Sales

Re: Anniston Advantage Program

Jack—Attached please find the letter that went to all Anniston original equipment truck manufacturers last week that your counterparts at Freeleaner and ZX wrote you about. As you can see, it is a pretty simple program open to all customers, doesn't lock out any of our competitors (as much as we'd love to be able to lock out Eden and ZX) and has drawn compliments from a couple of transit bus manufacturers. Given the take rate we expect, we'll still be making money so don't worry about your bonus.

I've also attached a slide presentation my guys put together when we finalized the program and just before the customer letters went out. Yes, you're right, I should have run it past you and your legal eagles beforehand but it didn't seem to raise any legal issues to me—still doesn't.

Once you and your experts have had a chance to review, let me know if you have any questions. Thanks.

Johnny H.

Anniston Advantage Program – Final Version

Presentation to John Hattley Staff

Judy Reinholm, Director Sales Strategy

Anniston Advantage – Background

- With collapse of sale to ZX, need to get back to marketing and sales and increasing automaticity
- While we "automatic guys" were distracted by merger talk, Eden was busy developing even cheaper – and better – manuals and selling them to "their" and "our" vocations
- We need to defend our turf, return the battle to their turf (where it was for years) and gear up again before ZX has a chance to re-start sales

Possible Elements of a Program

- Just for a limited time – one year – to allow our customers to readjust to Aniston still part of Grand, not ZX
- Our new Global Transmission had reduced our cost disadvantage to manuals but the new Eden manual has restored it – so need to quickly reduce our costs (or price?!?)
- Beat ZX back into the game and keep them where they are

Loyalty Program?

- Boat engine manufacturers and others have successfully used "loyalty programs" to solidify their shares and get some certainty on volumes
  - Kind of like a frequent flyer program
  - Customer free to go elsewhere – but incentive to stay "loyal"
- Can be used to conquest vocations and customers as well as defend them

Strawman

- Here are the details run past Financial:
  - Offer to all truck manufacturer customers
    - Exclude military and part sales to protect profit
  - For all their current vocations, must hit 50% automaticity to get discount
  - For all automatic purchases, must hit 90% Anniston to get discount
  - Discount is 20% on all purchases
    - Will need way to get discounts back if don't end up hitting targets

Reaction

- Offer to all?
  - If don't, some of our most loyal customers for years will scream
  - The couple OE's that only make school buses get a "windfall" – but they'd been talking about buying some or some more ZX's
- 20% too rich?
  - That's the level necessary to better Eden's improvements and get attention of end users
  - Finance says overall we'd still make money, given expected take rate by customers and extra sales in some "manual vocations" (and military and parts)

Effects on Selected Customers

- Expect all the OE's who only make transit and school buses and big garbage trucks to grab it
  - Might mean that ZX loses some sales but we don't have capacity to do 100% of all those OE's plus the other expected sales
- Bulldog likely to take because already above 50/90 on transit and garbage and close to 50 on their other vocations

Effects on Selected Customers (contin.)

- Freeleaner will have a tough choice because they're in so many vocations but would be a great win for us
  - Above 50% automatic on transit and garbage but well below 90% Anniston on both
    - Big ZX customer – maybe biggest?
  - About 20-30% on their three other vocations
    - Have used Edens for years and sell on price
  - But if Bulldog and the bus OE's take it, will Freeleaner feel "forced" to take?

Effects on Anniston

- Reduce profit but still make money, given expected take rate, sales increase and military and parts
- Helps jumpstart the renewed push for automaticity and counters moves by Eden
- Makes it more difficult for ZX to grow, especially with the best customers
  - We can't service 100% of all customers but pretty close
  - ZX might end up with sales even lower than today's
- Gives us better handle on our likely volumes (assuming expected take rates and expected truck sales)

Recommendation

- Institute a one-year loyalty program with terms as described
- Name of program: Anniston Advantage Program

CHAPTER 5

MONOPOLIZATION THROUGH REFUSALS TO DEAL

I. INTRODUCTION

The law of monopolization is the most controversial area of antitrust law. Other areas can generate debates over application of a specific set of facts but most antitrust practitioners agree on the law. Not so with monopolization. At most, antitrust courts and lawyers agree on a two-part test before finding a violation of Sherman Act Section 2: First, the defendant must be a "monopolist," usually defined as having a high market share and the ability to raise prices; and second, the monopolist must be "monopolizing," that is, taking inappropriate steps to maintain that monopoly. It is the second part of the test that creates the most controversy because courts do not want to condemn hard competition that is good for consumers.

There is no single test for "monopolization"; instead, courts and theorists have developed several tests depending on the actions being taken by a monopolist. Often those actions include various refusals to deal with a rival that harm that rival's ability to compete. This chapter reviews the tests used by courts to determine when such refusals amount to monopolization. Chapter 4 reviews the tests used to determine any limits on discounting placed on a monopolist.

The simulation exercise in this chapter gives you an opportunity to: review the terms of a research joint venture among two competitors; understand more about the industry of those two competitors through a magazine article; review emails, both internal and between the competitors, that explain the opposing views of why the joint effort ended and what the results might be; and use these materials provided and the cases discussed herein to practice organizing and holding a meeting with opposing counsel.

II. AN OVERVIEW OF THE LAW

Sherman Act Section 2 is the attempt by the antitrust laws to prevent unilateral action that causes harm to competition. Literally, the statute makes a felon of "every person who shall monopolize, or attempt to monopolize ... any part of the trade or commerce among the several States, or with foreign nations." The key term is "monopolize," a verb, instead of "monopolist," a noun. Only monopolists who monopolize violate Section 2. As the Supreme Court has said, the offense "has two elements: (1) the possession of monopoly power in the relevant market and (2) the willful acquisition or maintenance of that power, as distinguished from growth or development as a consequence of a superior product, business acumen or historic accident." *U.S. v. Grinnell Corp.*, 384 U.S. 563, 570–571 (1966). Other jurisdictions around the globe apply similar two part tests to their unilateral conduct statutes.

The first element, often described as "monopoly power," can be difficult to prove in any particular matter but, theoretically, is the element where there is widespread agreement. In most cases, the proof consists of a high market share in a relevant market plus evidence of the ability to price without regard to the price set by any competitors. Determining market shares, of course, requires the determination of the relevant product and geographic markets. Fortunately, antitrust courts and enforcers have developed robust methods for defining product markets. The Supreme Court expressed a rough version of the test decades ago in "the Cellophane case" when it described the search for all substitute products as follows: [whether products are substitutes and therefore in the same market] "depends on how different from one another are the offered commodities in character or use, [and] how far buyers will go to substitute on commodity for another ... [and whether they are] reasonably interchangeable by consumers for the same purpose." *U.S. v. E.I. duPont de Nemours & Co.*, 351 U.S. 377, 393 (1956). Since the opinion in the Cellophane case, antitrust enforcers have developed a more precise process for product and geographic market definition in merger reviews, although the process is used for other antitrust purposes as well. That process has been updated and published several times in the *Horizontal Merger Guidelines* published by the Federal Trade Commission and Department of Justice Antitrust Division. Under the *Guidelines*, enforcers or a court should begin with the narrowest definition of a product market and assume a monopolist. Then, the monopolist is assumed to impose a "small but significant non-transitory increase in price" and the reaction of consumers is estimated. If enough consumers would start buying a different product such that the price increase would not be profitable for the hypothetical monopolist, that other product is added to the market definition and the process is repeated. The same iterative process is used to determine the relevant geographic market as well.

Once the market is determined, historical sales data or expert estimates are used to derive the market share of the alleged "monopolist." While a market share of one hundred percent is not necessary to show monopoly power, courts have not set a specific lower threshold. The Supreme Court has said that a 75% share would have constituted a monopoly in *U.S. v. E.I. duPont de Nemours & Co.*, 351 U.S. 377, 391 (1956). Lower courts have rarely found monopoly power with a share lower than 50%. Even in cases with shares above 50%, determination of a high market share usually is not the end of the analysis; instead, courts then search for other evidence to confirm that the defendant has some ability to raise prices without fear of rival retaliation. A finding of monopoly power is more likely when the few remaining competitors are unlikely to expand output and potential competitors are unlikely to overcome barriers to entry in response to a price increase by a monopolist.

The second element of a Section 2 claim—monopolization—has been much more controversial both in theory and in application to any particular set of facts. The requirement even has several names: monopolization, exclusionary conduct, anticompetitive conduct, monopoly maintenance. Courts, academics, commissions and enforcers have spent years trying to develop an overall description that would prevent such "monopolization" without stopping tough competitive behavior beneficial to consumers. Those efforts have been unsuccessful. Therefore, courts instead have used a category approach, developing tests for different categories of conduct to determine when it rises to "monopolization." For allegations of an anticompetitive refusal to deal with a rival, courts recently have narrowed the times when they will depart from the usual rule and require a competitor to deal with a rival.

The rule that a company can choose with whom it does business was first recognized in *U.S. v. Colgate*, 250 U.S. 300 (1919). There, the defendant faced charges of vertical price fixing by refusing to sell its products to distributors that did not resell its products at its desired price. The Court stated:

> In the absence of any purpose to create or maintain a monopoly, the [antitrust laws do] not restrict the long-recognized right of trade or manufacturer engaged in an entirely private business, freely to exercise his own independent discretion as to parties with whom he will deal.

While *Colgate* is a Sherman Act Section 1 case, subsequent courts have taken from the second part of the quote a general principle that private parties will not be forced to deal with others, including competitors. It is the first part of the quote—"In the absence of any purpose to create or maintain a monopoly"—that must be interpreted under Sherman Section 2 to determine when the usual *Colgate* rule will be ignored and a special duty to deal with its rival will be imposed on a monopolist.

The Court found such a duty in *Otter Tail Power Co. v. U.S.*, 410 U.S. 366 (1973). Otter Tail was an electric company that created its own electricity, wheeled it over its own wires and then distributed it at retail. While there were other entities that distributed electricity at the retail level (including municipal systems), Otter Tail was the only source of electricity in many geographic markets. When Otter Tail was replaced at the retail level, it refused to wheel its electricity to the new retailer. There was no technical reason for such refusal, according to the Court. Where Otter Tail had never supplied the electricity at retail, it did wheel its electricity to the retailer. Otter Tail claimed that because its regulator, the Federal Power Commission, did not order it to interconnect with its retail competitors, it did not violate Sherman Act Section 2. The Court disagreed, finding that while the regulatory scheme did not turn Otter Tail into a common carrier required to deal with all parties, it did still require Otter Tail to comply with the antitrust laws. Here, the Court found the record "abundantly clear" that Otter Tail used its monopoly power to "foreclose competition or gain a competitive advantage, or to destroy a competitor, all in violation of [Section 2]." *Otter Tail*, at 377.

The Court found another exception to the usual *Colgate* rule in *Aspen Skiing Co. v. Aspen Highlands Skiing Corp.*, 472 U.S. 585 (1985). The defendant, Ski Co., operated three of the four ski locations in Aspen. Highlands operated the other location. For years, the two companies had cooperated on a popular joint "all Aspen ticket" that allowed customers to ski at any of the four locations. For reasons that did not make it into the record before the Court, Ski Co. ended the joint effort and thwarted Highlands' efforts to come close to replicating it. While the Court acknowledged that "even a firm with monopoly power has no duty to engage in joint marketing with a competitor," it also explained that a decision to end such a joint marketing effort may "have evidentiary significance." Here the Court saw no valid business reason for Ski Co.'s termination of a successful joint marketing effort and, therefore, characterized the decision as exclusionary conduct that violated Section 2.

Aspen Skiing has remained a controversial decision and has attracted plenty of critics, including the Court itself in *Verizon Communications v. Law Offices of Curtis v. Trinko*, 540 U.S. 398 (2004). In that case, the Court placed *Aspen Skiing* "at or near the outer boundary of Section 2 liability" and distinguished it from the facts of *Trinko*. *Aspen Skiing*, at 409. Verizon was the incumbent local exchange carrier in certain geographic areas and, like all such carriers after the Telecommunications Act of 1996, had a duty to deal with its competitors in the phone market. Verizon was accused of providing those services only slowly. Trinko was a customer of one of those Verizon competitors and he claimed this delay was a Section 2 violation. The Court saw two reasons why, unlike as in *Aspen Skiing* and *Otter Tail*, it could not conclude that Verizon's actions were exclusionary. First, Verizon was not terminating a voluntary—and presumably profitable—course of dealing with a rival as the defendant had in *Aspen Skiing*; here, it had never dealt in this way with its rivals and showed no desire to do so until forced by the statute. Second, Verizon was not refusing to sell to its rival some product or service that it sold to others. In *Aspen Skiing*, the defendant refused to even sell its lift tickets to the plaintiff for cash in order to thwart any attempts to replicate the all Aspen pass. In *Otter Tail*, the defendant sold electricity to retailers where it had never had the retail business before but refused to sell to its retail replacements. As a result of *Trinko*, it seems clear that a refusal to deal by a monopolist will not be held to be exclusionary conduct unless such a refusal is irrational in the absence of an anticompetitive motive. What is not clear is whether the Court would make such a finding only if the facts are exactly like *Aspen Skiing* or *Otter Tail*.

The Court was even more skeptical of a similar claim—a "price squeeze" by a monopolist—in *Pacific Bell Telephone Co. v. linkLine Communications*, 555 U.S. 438 (2009). The price squeeze claim arises where the defendant sells a product or service—such as DSL service here—at "too high" a price at the wholesale level and "too low" a price at the retail level. The result is that any competitor is "squeezed" in the middle and unable to compete. Here, the Court refused to view price squeezes as unitary claims but instead reviewed both the wholesale and retail components. The Court applied *Trinko* to find the wholesale pricing component lawful: Because there was no separate antitrust duty of the defendant to deal with its rivals at all, there was no duty for it to deal with them at a particular price. As for the retail level, the Court applied *Brooke Group* and found that the plaintiff could not meet its stringent two-part test of below cost pricing and possible recoupment. (See Chapter 4 for further explanation of *Brooke Group*.) In sum, the Court found "[t]wo wrong claims do not make one that is right" and rejected the price squeeze claim. *linkLine*, at 457.

III. BACKGROUND

There are two companies in the U.S. that offer roadside assistance services through motor vehicle manufacturers, insurance companies or others: Criss Cross Country (CCC) and Tows R Us (TOW). The two companies connect tow truck operators; companies that offer "roadside assistance" like car manufacturers and insurance companies; and customers stuck on the side of the road.

When a covered motorist has a breakdown, he calls a phone number provided by his car or insurance company. That call actually goes to a CCC or TOW call center agent who takes down the information and then attempts to locate a tow operator local to the customer who has agreed to be part of the CCC or TOW network. CCC and TOW have been the two main competitors for years and CCC currently has about 60% of the "market" with TOW holding the rest. Until recently, some tow operators had agreements to be part of both the CCC and TOW networks; however, in the last several months, CCC has moved away from the industry-standard one year non-exclusive agreement to five year exclusive agreements. It has been difficult but TOW has been able to find other tow operators, although sometimes the quality has not been quite as good.

Also, CCC has developed and is beginning to implement a new software system, Virtual Dispatch, that will change the way tow operators are dispatched. Instead of the CCC agent looking at a list of tow operators; calling the shop of the one who looks to be closest; then maybe following up with a secondary cell phone number to the tow operator; providing the customer info over the phone; and then waiting for the tow operator to confirm that he is with the customer or for the customer to call back complaining about waiting on the side of the road, Virtual Dispatch automates many of those steps. The CCC agent inputs the customer's location and locates it on a computer screen; locates the exact location of the nearest tow truck, not just the shop, through the use of a GPS/communications system provided by CCC and placed in each truck at CCC's expense; sends the customer information to the truck's GPS system electronically; and then updates the customer with real time information as the tow operator drives to the customer.

CCC has developed the system, including the software, by itself and has started to provide the GPS/communications units, free of charge, to all its tow operators who sign the five year exclusive agreement. CCC and TOW signed a memorandum of understanding that CCC would explore allowing TOW to utilize Virtual Dispatch if the two parties could agree on the basics of the system and if TOW agreed to cover certain initial costs. Recently, about the time CCC started signing the five year agreements with tow operators and placing the GPS/communications units, it invoked a provision in the memorandum of understanding and broke off discussions with TOW about use of the system. Specifically, the CCC and TOW signatories to the MOU exchanged emails to formally end the joint research effort. TOW has contacted CCC since then to try to re-start the joint effort or otherwise gain access to the system, most recently armed with documents from a syndicate of banks to show its ability to pay for its share of the cost of the system, all to no avail. CCC's market share has started to edge up, a few percentage points in the last few months.

Getting You Back On the Road Again Can Be Good Business

By BM Staff Reporter Stephanie Hart

It's a terrible feeling. You're stuck on the side of the road in some different city with a dead car. But wait—you suddenly remember that you have roadside assistance available to you—maybe from your car's manufacturer, maybe from your insurance company or some other group to which you belong. So you make the call and suddenly—or maybe not so suddenly—a tow truck arrives and gets you back on the road.

No matter how you obtained that roadside assistance, when you make that call there's a very good chance that you'll be talking to representatives of one of two companies: Criss Cross Country (CCC) or Tows R Us (TOW). Most providers of such roadside assistance services outsource those services—who can be bothered to know the right tow truck operator in Muskegon or Moline? And CCC and TOW are the only two companies that provide those services.

CCC is the long-time incumbent, having practically started the business over thirty years ago. TOW is considered the upstart, although it has been in business for more than a decade. Both companies are privately-held—and notoriously private—but all indications are that both are very profitable. While it is extremely time-consuming to set up a network of tow truck operators, it doesn't cost nearly as much to use and maintain it. So when some company or group wants to offer the service, they almost have no choice other than CCC and TOW—and BM is told that the two companies seem to understand the situation and price accordingly.

Neither company offered up statements or answers to questions for this report; however, several companies and tow truck operators were willing to discuss the industry, though usually off the record for fear of offending one or both of the only two players.

CCC has been the market leader for as long as anyone can remember. Its historical share of the market is estimated by those sources as around 60%, although that figure might have edged up a few percentage points in the last six months or so. TOW has consistently been nipping at CCC's heels, never quite stealing away and holding on to enough accounts to catch their long-time rivals.

The logistics of setting up the business can be daunting. Companies that offer these services will want assurances that there are no major holes in coverage across the country. After all, an insurance company will be embarrassed, at least, if one of its customers from Los Angeles breaks down in Tucson and is told the closest tow truck is in Phoenix. So CCC and TOW have contracts with at least one tow truck operator in every major—and many not-so-major—metropolitan area across the country. That's a lot of contracts.

But then when a stranded motorist dials the number given her, she is connected to a call center operator for one of the companies. That operator will answer the call with the name of the insurance or car company that hired CCC or TOW—that's why you've never heard of them. That operator then obtains location information from the driver, checks a database for the closest tow operator and passes on the location information. And voila, the driver is rescued.

Except it doesn't always work so smoothly. Sometimes the location information isn't quite right or gets garbled in the communication to the tow truck. Or the tow truck operator is rude or otherwise offensive to the motorist. So while CCC and TOW have their networks in place, they can't and don't rest on their laurels. Both are constantly following up on complaints of slow or otherwise poor service and making sure the actual drivers—who turn over about every six months—get enough training to know how to both drive the truck and calm a frazzled motorist. The tow operators BM contacted thought CCC had the more stringent standards.

CCC also seems to be taking the lead in trying to use modern technology to fix some of the known issues in the industry. Several sources talked about CCC's new Virtual Dispatch system. Instead of guessing which tow operator might be closest to the stranded motorist, CCC personnel will be able to view a real time map of all the tow trucks in the same general area to see which one is best situated to handle this matter. The vehicle location information is then transmitted electronically to that truck and the call center operator can "watch" the truck get closer to the disabled vehicle. All this technical assistance is done through a combination GPS/tablet that CCC insists that its tow operators have in every truck. So if you ask, the operator at least will know if the truck is expected to reach you in ten minutes or two hours.

Our sources had heard rumblings that TOW was going to help pay for the Virtual Dispatch system and get a chance to use it as well. We now hear, however, that CCC told TOW about six months ago that it was going to keep the system for itself. Because about a year ago TOW had scrapped the similar system it had been working on, it now is once again playing catch up. CCC is now signing long term, usually five years, contracts with the best tow operators in each city and installing the GPS/tablet for free. Our sources differ on whether these industry developments are responsible for CCC's recent uptick in share.

One thing is clear—there won't be any competition besides TOW for CCC anytime soon. Some of the better tow truck operators understand those dynamics and have switched to CCC or dropped TOW when they have relationships with both. It remains to be seen if CCC can "drive TOW off the road."

MEMORANDUM OF UNDERSTANDING

This AGREEMENT is between Criss Cross Country Inc., a corporation organized under the laws of Delaware ("CCC"), and Tows R U.S. Operating LLC, a limited liability company organized under the laws of Michigan ("TOW")(collectively "Parties").

WHEREAS the Parties are both engaged in the business of providing roadside assistance services on a private label basis to various companies that serve millions of motorists;

WHEREAS as part of the provision of those roadside assistance services, each of the Parties must facilitate communications among motorists, Party call center personnel and tow truck operators (plus, in special circumstances, other entities such as local law enforcement personnel)(collectively, "the Communications");

WHEREAS each of the Parties has taken steps to explore technologically advanced methods of the Communications with the goal of providing these roadside assistance services with higher quality and lower costs;

WHEREAS TOW acknowledges that CCC's efforts to explore these technologically advanced methods are further along than TOW's; and

WHEREAS the parties wish to explore if their respective research efforts can be combined in a way such that each Party will reduce its costs of researching or implementing such advanced forms of the Communications and/or each Party will be able to provide even better roadside assistance services to motorists than either could individually ("the Project").

THEREFORE, the Parties do hereby agree as follows:

1. **Elements to be Explored During the Project.** While the Parties have reason to believe that their respective research efforts on advanced forms of the Communication are similar and that combining them will be beneficial to each Party and their respective customers and served motorists, the Parties will test that belief during the Project. CCC also has concerns about TOW's ability to make the payments described in Paragraph 2 of this Agreement. While TOW thinks such concerns are unfounded, TOW agrees to discuss that issue with CCC as part of the Project.

2. **TOW Payment to CCC.** CCC has been working on its research of advanced forms of the Communications for longer than has TOW. The Parties believe CCC's efforts are much closer to fruition and will be the basis of any combined advanced form of the Communications that the Parties might develop. Therefore, part of the Project will also include the appropriate amount and form of compensation to be paid by TOW to CCC to compensate CCC for the extra work that it is bringing to the potential combined advanced form of the Communications.

3. **No Commitment to Proceed and No Final Agreement.** Each of the Parties acknowledges and understands that this Agreement does not obligate either Party to proceed with a combined version of the advanced form of the Communications, no matter what the results of the Project might be. In addition, each of the Parties acknowledges and understands that neither this Agreement nor any document generated as part of the Project will constitute a final agreement related to the joint development and implementation of the advanced forms of the Communications.

4. **Confidentiality.** The existence of this Agreement and the Project will be kept confidential by each of the Parties. Only those Party personnel and advisers who have a need to know about the Agreement or the Project will be told.

5. **No Licenses.** Each Party agrees that it will use any information received from the other Party only for purposes of the Project. No licenses to any intellectual property, whether protected by copyright, patent or trademark, are being granted in this Agreement. Any Party remains free to use outside of the Project any information that is not protected intellectual property and that the Party can show was known or became known to that Party prior to or outside the Project.

6. **Term and Termination.** This Agreement will last for three months and can be extended by the mutual agreement of the Parties for another six months. Neither Party is obligated for any reason to agree to any extension of this Agreement. In addition, either Party may terminate this Agreement immediately and at any time and for any reason or no reason at all by notifying the signatory of the other Party by a letter or electronic mail.

7. **Expenses.** Each Party will be responsible for its own expenses of any type that are incurred implementing this Agreement.

8. **Merger and Modification**. This Agreement represents the complete agreement of the Parties on this topic. No other earlier or later communications of the Parties, whether verbal or in writing, shall be deemed to modify the terms of this Agreement. This Agreement may not be modified except by a written amendment of its terms approved by personnel at the Party having authority to enter joint research agreements.

This Agreement is entered into on the later of the dates listed below.

_____   _____

On behalf of CCC   On behalf of TOW

_____   _____

Name   Name

_____   _____

Title   Title

_____   _____

Date   Date

[TOW Email]

From: Chris Perry <perryc@tow.com>

To: Anthony Thomas <athomas@cccountry.com>

Re: Re: Termination of Research Agreement

Anthony—thanks for the courtesy of the email below, much appreciated. As I said on the phone, CCC's decision to try to terminate this Agreement caught us here at TOW by surprise. We thought we'd been making good progress and, to use your words, were almost on the same page and seeing eye to eye. Also, we don't understand the sudden concern about our financial condition—as I told you yesterday, we're doing just fine but we're having our CPA and banker put something down on a piece of paper that we think will convince you.

Some here have suggested that your attempt to terminate might have something to do with what's happening in the marketplace. The thinking is that some of your recent success at snapping up great operators means you don't think you need us—and our ideas and volume—anymore. Since we've pretty much abandoned our own original research in this area, this move by you puts us in a pretty tough spot. Unless you reconsider, we'll have to take a look at all our options.

Hope you understand—thanks.

Chris

Christine A. Perry
TOW, LLC

> [Criss Cross Country Email]
>
> **From:** Anthony Thomas <athomas@cccountry.com>
>
> **To:** Chris Perry <perryc@tow.com>
>
> **Re:** Termination of Research Agreement
>
> Chris—
>
> I'm writing to confirm what I just told you over the phone. CCC is hereby terminating the MOU regarding the research into the advanced form of communications that you and I signed five months ago. We already extended the agreement once and we just don't think it makes sense to go any further. My lawyer says I don't have to give a reason but I think you deserve to know our thinking. We're just don't think that our two great companies are on the same page on how to do these advanced communications technically and we don't see eye to eye on rolling it out. Also, as I told you on the phone, there is some concern about whether TOW has the ability to reimburse us for the extra research we'd be bringing to the project.
>
> I think we and our teams gave it a great try but now is the time to go our separate ways on this issue. Thanks
>
> A.

CHAPTER 6

MERGERS

I. INTRODUCTION

This chapter explores the antitrust treatment of mergers and similar transactions. Such transactions are reviewed under Clayton Act Section 7 and are to be judged anticompetitive and, therefore, illegal where they "may . . . substantially . . . lessen competition." Up until the mid-1970s, this provision was used by courts to prevent most mergers between horizontal competitors. Since that time, however, most horizontal mergers have been allowed to proceed as the substantive standards became much more lenient. At about the same time, the procedure through which mergers were reviewed changed drastically. The Hart-Scott-Rodino Act (HSR) required merging parties to seek permission from the federal antitrust agencies before consummating a merger. As a result, the decision of those agencies has become the final decision in almost all mergers and very few are pursued in court.

The simulation exercise in this chapter gives you an opportunity to: review a small selection of documents normally produced under HSR by companies contemplating a merger to determine if the proposed transaction raises significant antitrust concerns; explore ways to edit those documents, if given the opportunity, to better explain the likely effects of the transaction to any subsequent antitrust reviewers; and use those documents to conduct a mock meeting between counsel for the merging parties and the antitrust officials.

II. AN OVERVIEW OF THE LAW

It was not necessary for antitrust law to move beyond Sherman Act Section 1 to cover mergers. After all, an agreement to merge between two parties can be an "agreement in restraint of trade." In fact, one of the claims against the defendant in *Standard Oil Co. of New Jersey v. United States,* 221 U.S. 1 (1911) was that it had used acquisitions and other corporate combinations to harm competition. Congress has thought on more than one occasion, however, that the courts were not interpreting the antitrust laws strictly enough to prevent what it deemed to be harmful mergers. To remedy that concern, the 1914 Clayton Act specifically covering mergers was passed and then significantly strengthened in 1950 by the Celler-Kefauver Act. The statute holds in pertinent part that "No person shall . . . acquire . . . assets of another person . . . where in any line of commerce or in any section of the country, the effect . . . may be substantially to lessen competition or tend to create a monopoly."

Judicial interpretations of the statute became quite strict in the 1960s. Courts, led by the Supreme Court, saw a Congressional "fear of what was considered to be a rising tide of economic concentration in the American economy." *Brown Shoe Co. v. United States,* 370 U.S. 294 (1962). That fear, along with the "may be" language in the statute, was used to prevent even mergers between small competitors in industries with many competitors so as to prevent "the lessening of competition . . . [while] still in its incipiency." *Id.* at 323. In some cases, the Court seemed to almost shift the burden of proof, stating that a merger resulting in a significant increase in competition was so likely to lessen competition, "it must be enjoined in the absence of evidence clearly" showing no anticompetitive effects. *United States v. Philadelphia National Bank,* 374 U.S. 321 (1965). Even during this era, however, the Court still proclaimed a desire to "protect competition, not competitors" and prevent only those mergers that posed a reasonable probability, not mere possibility, of harming competition. *Brown Shoe,* at 323. The result was the blocking of many, but not all, mergers, often among small competitors, without a clear consensus as to the rationale.

Perhaps no case exemplifies all these issues as well as *United States v. Von's Grocery*, 384 U.S. 270 (1966). There, the Court found anticompetitive the merger between two grocery store chains with a combined 7.5% share of the retail grocery market in Los Angeles. The majority spent one sentence identifying the market but many paragraphs describing Congress's fear of rising concentration in the Celler-Kefauver Act. The majority found that incipient trend in the reduction of single grocery stores from approximately 5300 in 1950 to 3600 in 1963 and the increase in grocery chains from 96 to 150. The dissent, authored by Justice Stewart, took issue with the geographic market definition, finding that a "housewife's 10 minute driving time test" conducted by the Justice Department revealed that many of the stores of the parties were too far apart to effectively compete with each other. He also thought that the share of even the larger Los Angeles market overstated the merger's possible negative effect because of ongoing changes in that market, such as the number of firms exiting and entering the growing Los Angeles market. Finally, even Justice Stewart showed his confusion about the Court's merger jurisprudence, famously saying that "the sole consistency that I can find is that in litigation under [the Clayton Act], the Government always wins." *Von's*, at 301.

In the 1970s, both the substantive standard applied to mergers and the procedural details of merger review changed considerably. The change in the standard reflected new economic thinking that placed much less emphasis on competitor counts and market share trends and more emphasis on dynamic factors meant to better describe and predict competition in the market. The case generally described as the inflection point is *United States v. General Dynamics*, 415 U.S. 486 (1974). The Court, with Justice Stewart now writing for the majority, found the merger of two large coal producers not to be anticompetitive. The Court defined the product market as one for energy, not just for coal, by applying the price elasticity of demand concept to find that coal competed with gas and other sources of energy. Also, the Court found that the current market shares of the two parties did not provide an accurate prediction of future competition because one of the parties had such small reserves of coal that were not already committed to buyers.

The merger review procedure also drastically changed at this time with the passage of the Hart-Scott-Rodino Antitrust Improvements Act of 1976 (HSR). HSR requires that parties to most large acquisitions file a form and certain documents with the two federal antitrust agencies and await approval before consummating the transaction. HSR's goal was to provide advance notice of large, potentially anticompetitive mergers to the antitrust agencies so they could more readily review them and sue to block those that posed competition concerns. That goal has been met; administration of the program by the FTC, however, has had many other consequences as well. While the overwhelming majority of the transactions filed are quickly approved, many more transactions than were originally envisioned must be filed. The result is extra cost for those transactions, both in terms of delays of at least a few weeks plus the costs to prepare the filing package and pay the six-figure filing fee. For transactions that must be investigated further, those costs can increase to many months of delay and millions of dollars in costs to make submissions that rival those in large litigation. In addition, HSR inspired more than one hundred other jurisdictions to pass their own similar—but far from identical—premerger notification systems.

The regulations implementing HSR are complicated and have changed since the statute's passage but have always required filings for transactions by parties that met certain size criteria. Those criteria are now adjusted for inflation. As of 2019, transactions valued at less than $90M require no filings while all those valued at approximately $360M or more must be filed, absent any exemptions. Those transaction in between must be filed if either the buyer or seller has $180M in assets or sales and the other's figures meet or exceed $18M. If the thresholds are met, then both parties must complete a form that describes the transaction and the filing party in some detail. In addition, certain documents relied on by the party's officers or directors to approve the transaction must be turned in. The buyer must also pay a six-figure filing fee based on the size of the transaction.

Once the filings are received, the two antitrust agencies have thirty days to decide which agency will review the transaction and to choose one of these options: allow the transaction to proceed, perhaps even by making an "early termination" of the waiting period; or require the parties to respond to a "second request" for information to make a better informed decision. To choose between those options, the agency will seek additional information from the parties, suppliers, customers or anyone expert in the industry. The parties have a large incentive to voluntarily comply with those requests: if the agency feels it must make a "second request," the result for the parties will be months more of delay and discovery. (That scenario is the subject of the exercise in this chapter.) Once the agency has received the complete response to the "second request," it may allow the transaction to proceed or seek a court injunction preventing its consummation. Often during the course of the compliance with the second request, the parties and the agency are able to negotiate modifications to the transaction—such as selling off certain assets to a third party to preserve competition—that meet the concerns of the agency and the desires of the parties.

Few parties are willing to endure the further delay and expense from fighting an agency challenge even at a preliminary injunction hearing; therefore, most parties abandon any challenged transaction. The result is that few mergers have generated court opinions since HSR's passage and there have been no Supreme Court merger decisions in decades. Instead, the ultimate decisions on most mergers are now made by officials at one of the two federal antitrust agencies, usually after working with Washington, D.C. outside counsel representing the parties.

To assist parties in understanding the analysis to be used to evaluate their transactions, the agencies have issued several iterations of merger review guidelines. Each generation of guidelines has been progressively more sophisticated—and more complicated—than the prior one as it incorporated the latest economic thinking on the competitive effects of mergers. The guidelines are not statutes or regulations and do not have the force of law; however, because they are the product of experts in the area, most of the few courts that have reviewed merger cases since 1976 have found them very persuasive. Certainly, the merger analysis by any modern court will be much more informed by these guidelines than by the analysis used in a case like *Von's*. Almost all of the most recent versions of the guidelines have contained the same five basic steps. (The 2010 version did say that the agencies might concentrate only on the "competitive effects" stage and skip defining a market in appropriate circumstances; however, the merger challenges by the agencies since 2010 have followed all five steps.) First, the agencies will try to determine the product and geographic markets affected by the merger through an iterative process of predicting where consumers might turn if prices in the hypothetical market were raised a small but significant amount. Second, the market shares of the participants in those markets are determined and the concentration of the market before and after the merger is calculated. Third, given all the current market facts, the agencies try to predict the competitive effects of the merger. Potential anticompetitive effects include the ability of the merged firm to successfully raise prices on its own or in conjunction with any remaining competitors. Fourth, the agencies consider the possibility that some new competitor not currently in the affected markets would enter in such a way that any anticompetitive effects from the merger would be mitigated. Finally, the agencies consider whether the merger is necessary to create any efficiencies that might change the dynamics of the market so that, again, any anticompetitive effects would be mitigated.

A good example of the application of an earlier version of this analysis—and one of the few post-HSR court decisions—is the district court's opinion in *FTC v. Staples*, 970 F. Supp. 1066 (D.D.C. 1997). The court granted the FTC's motion and enjoined the merger of Staples and Office Depot. The court agreed with the FTC's contention that the proper product market was "consumable office supplies sold through office superstores." The court accepted that market definition because the internal documents of the parties seemed to show that the parties focused on each other and OfficeMax to the exclusion of other sellers; office supply superstores looked different and were recognized as being different by customers; and the prices at the parties' stores generally were lower in geographic areas where all three superstores were present than in areas where only two or one competed. The court feared that such pricing patterns would only worsen after the merger. Entry into the market was unlikely because of the time and capital needed to establish a successful network of such superstores. Finally, while the efficiencies claimed by the parties were absolutely large, the court found them relatively small because they could easily be offset by even a small price increase after the merger.

III. BACKGROUND

Grand Motors Corporation has decided to sell its Anniston Transmission Division (ATD). To help it in the sale process, Grand hired an investment bank to prepare a confidential information memorandum (CIM). That CIM was prepared by bankers with the help of the industry experts at ATD. The CIM was then shared with all prospective, legitimate bidders. As with all CIMs, it provides very good background on the business being sold on topics such as product, competition, and history. As such, it is almost certain to be turned into the agencies as part of any HSR process.

Grand and its investment bankers were able to negotiate a sale of ATD to ZX ("Zed Ex"). As detailed in the CIM, both ATD and ZX make automatic transmissions that go into certain medium and heavy duty trucks. These sizes of trucks include the delivery trucks in town as well as the line-haul tractors attached to trailers on the highway. As described in the CIM, there are two types of transmissions that go into these size trucks and the other, much more prevalent, kind is a manual transmission. Eden is the largest manufacturer of manuals—actually, the largest for any transmissions that go into these size trucks. There are four other makers of manuals and none of the transmissions that go into light duty trucks, like pickups, or cars would fit these size trucks.

ZX and Grand have filed HSR forms and the requisite documents. Those documents include short presentations that were made to the respective Boards of Directors and two emails from the ATD engineering and sales directors to the ATD President regarding the possible effects of the merger. The parties have continued to collect information and documents in anticipation of subsequent requests from the reviewing agency. The agency, here the Antitrust Division of the Department of Justice, has started its job by reviewing the HSR submissions and contacting others who might be interested in the transaction, such as truck manufacturers and truck buyers. The agency has not decided yet if a "second request" for information will be necessary to complete its task.

Confidential Management Briefing Book

for

Anniston Transmission Division

of

Grand Motors Corporation

Prepared by PJ Stanklin Mogan Partners

Introduction

The Anniston Transmission Division of Grand Motors Corporation is the world's leading producer of automatic transmissions for medium and heavy duty trucks, buses and other commercial and military vehicles. Founded by James A. Anniston in Westerville Ohio in 1915, Anniston was purchased by Grand after Anniston's death in 1928 because of its expertise in components for the aviation and trucking industries. Anniston developed a transmission for large tracked vehicles, including tanks, during World War II. After the war, Anniston began to focus on transmissions for medium and heavy commercial and military vehicles and developed the first automatic transmissions for such vehicles in 1947. The company has been consistently profitable for decades as it single-handedly increased the automaticity of these types of vehicles in every vocation. Look under any modern transit bus in the United States today, for instance, and you are almost certain to find an Anniston Automatic.

Grand Motors Corporation has decided to explore strategic options for its Anniston Transmission Division so Grand can focus on its core competency of producing great light duty cars and trucks.

Product

Transmissions transfer power from a motor vehicle's engine through a driveline to the wheels. The two most commonly-used transmission types are automatics and manuals. Automatic transmissions use a torque converter to change gears automatically in response to changes in engine speed. Manual transmissions require drivers to change gears, usually through the use of a mechanical clutch and gear selector.

Automatics and manuals have different characteristics. Automatics require no special driver training and provide a smoother ride with minimal driver effort. Manuals, though usually about half the price of automatics, require more driver skill, attention and, especially in medium and heavy-duty vehicles, strength. Most light-duty vehicles, especially personal use vehicles, use automatics. The majority of medium and heavy-duty vehicles use manuals although, as described below, automatics have made great inroads in certain vocations.

Anniston makes automatic transmissions exclusively. Anniston's current product line-up only goes in medium and heavy-duty vehicles. The new Global Transmission includes a model capable of being used in the heaviest light-duty trucks, such as certain full-size pickup trucks, as well as trucks sold in Europe and elsewhere.

Vocations

Anniston has taken a two-pronged approach in its successful attempt to increase the use of automatic transmissions in medium and heavy-duty vehicles. First, it has worked with truck manufacturers to ensure that Anniston transmissions work smoothly behind the many engines that power these vehicles. Anniston's sales force has worked directly with the largest truck manufacturers to explain the benefits of automaticity while its independent distributors have spread the word among the many smaller, local manufacturers. Second, Anniston's marketing team has spent considerable time with the buyers and end users of these vehicles to show them the greater ease and safety that automatics bring to every vocation. The years spent demonstrating Anniston Automatics to local transit authorities, government procurement officials and other fleet buyers mean that some drivers can "no longer imagine living without an Anniston."

The result of decades of work is that an increasing number of uses—called "vocations" in the industry—use an increasing number of automatics, usually Anniston Automatics. For instance, nearly all transit buses sold in the U.S. in the last several years have been equipped with an automatic transmission and approximately 75% of those transmissions were Anniston Automatics. The Anniston "People Transportation" segment of the Sales and Marketing Staff worked with Anniston Engineering, bus manufacturers and local transit officials to tweak Anniston Automatics to allow these heavy vehicles to move smoothly and efficiently in stop-and-go traffic with minimal driver training and superior passenger comfort. The result was approximately 3000 Anniston Automatics, nearly $38M worth, sold for use in transit buses last year.

Similarly, the Anniston "Waste Removal" Sale and Marketing personnel have worked for many years to convince purchasers and users of heavy refuse route trucks of the benefits of Anniston Automatics. These trucks collect refuse on defined routes and are constantly stopping and starting to perform their responsibilities. The benefits to the drivers—and the private or municipal owners—are obvious. The result is that almost all the trucks in the heavy refuse route truck segment use automatics and 80% of them (2500 or $25M last year) are Anniston Automatics.

Sales and Marketing Results

The results of the Anniston marketing efforts show in the steadily increasing automaticity of the medium and heavy truck segment. Ten years ago, only 15% of the transmissions in these vehicles sold that year contained an automatic. Last year, that figure had climbed to 25%, as detailed below, and shows no signs of stopping.

Transmissions in Medium and Heavy Vehicles in the U.S. Last Year

Anniston Automatics	22,000
ZX Automatics	2,500
JD Voin Automatics	500
Manuals (Several mfrs)	75,000

For several vocations, automatic transmissions have become the transmission of choice in the U.S. For instance, only Anniston and ZX sold transmissions used in heavy refuse route trucks last year. For transit buses, almost all the transmissions sold last year in the U.S. were made by Anniston or ZX with the small remainder being automatics by Voin. Finally, ninety percent of the school buses sold last year contained an automatic to safely move their "precious cargo" and 90% of those automatics were Anniston Automatics.

Future growth in the sale of Anniston Automatics in the U.S. is still an exciting probability as the economy grows, more users of these trucks recognize the benefits of automaticity and the smallest of Anniston's new line of transmissions competes for sales in the heaviest of the light duty pickups. With the new Global Transmission, however, Anniston is well-positioned to grow outside the U.S., especially in Europe where other automatic transmission providers have begun to extol the benefits of automaticity.

All these sales and marketing efforts have translated into impressive revenues and profits for Anniston. Last year, revenues were just over $220M and generated approximately $33M in profit. That 15% margin has grown three percentage points in the last ten years along with the growth in automaticity and remains higher than most other motor vehicle component suppliers.

Competitors

Anniston faces a limited number of competitors. Manufacturers of transmissions for light duty vehicles pose little competitive threat to Anniston for two main reasons. First, while the transmissions perform the same function as Anniston Automatics and contain similar components, they are not built to withstand the weight and heavy duty cycles of all medium and heavy vehicles. Second, most of the manufacturers of transmissions for light vehicles are the producers of light vehicles and only rarely sell transmissions to other vehicle producers.

Within the market for transmissions for medium and heavy vehicles, there are five producers of manual transmissions. The largest, Eden Transmissions, sold just over half the manual transmissions for medium and heavy vehicles last year. Each of the four remaining manual transmission suppliers saw their sales drop last year, even as sales of medium and heavy vehicles rose slightly, as the shares represented by Eden and the automatic producers rose. No new producers of manual transmissions for these vehicles have entered in over ten years.

ZX (pronounced "Zed Ex") is a German manufacturer of automatic transmissions for these vehicles that entered the U.S. market four years ago. ZX has concentrated its sales efforts on those vocations where automaticity is already quite high (in both the U.S. and Europe), especially transit buses and heavy refuse route trucks. ZX has recently completed a manufacturing facility in Chicago. JD Voin is also a German manufacturer and the only other supplier of automatics for these vehicles in Europe. Voin began exporting transmissions to the U.S. two years ago and has announced plans to build a production facility in Alabama in two years. The two producers of transmissions in Japan that could fit all but the heaviest of these trucks have made no announcements about any intention to enter the U.S. market.

Development of Global Transmission

Three years ago, Anniston took all it knew about the manufacture, development and application of these automatics— and improved it all. Anniston started by setting out to develop an entire line of transmissions that could perform with the well-known Anniston Automatic reliability in all the current vocations. Then, it worked on reducing both the manufacturing and lifetime cost of the transmissions, focusing especially on fuel savings. Finally, Anniston worked on expanding its product line for the first time into U.S. light vehicles and medium and heavy vehicles that met all the different requirements in Europe and Japan.

After three years and $150M, the result is a new line of Anniston Automatics called the Global Transmissions. Simply put, the Global Transmissions are the best Anniston Automatics yet. They bring all the benefits of automaticity expected from Anniston Automatics but in a better, more efficient and less expensive package that no competitor can touch. The Global Transmission has the capability to expand Anniston Automatics sales in vocations where automaticity is already high plus in new vocations, like some light vehicles, and other geographies. As one long-time Anniston Automatic user described it when taking ownership of a new heavy refuse route truck with a Global Transmission earlier this year, "Thanks—nobody else could have done this kind of development."

[Anniston Email]

From: William Clink, Anniston Chief Engineer

To: Bobbie Johnson, Anniston President and Grand Vice President

Subject: Confidential—Analysis of Potential Transaction

Bobbie—I have been involved with the negotiations and the due diligence the guys from ZX have been performing. You asked for a summary of my thoughts on engineering synergies if we were to combine with them. Here are my thoughts:

I have reviewed numerous ZX transmissions in teardowns and in service for years, even before they entered the U.S. market a few years ago. I've always been impressed. They show typical "German engineering," in that there are no obvious mistakes or problems. But they aren't typical "German engineers" in that their transmissions are not obviously too expensive.

Now that I've had a few chances to talk with my counterpart and some other ZX engineers (though not too many because the lawyers wouldn't let us), I'm even more impressed and excited about the possibility of putting our respective products and expertise together. In particular, I like what they've done with their heaviest transmission, the one that goes in heavy refuse trucks. It is lighter than ours—and, therefore, a little less expensive and much more fuel efficient. Ours has greater take-off capability, so ours can more quickly get the truck up to 15mph, which is all a refuse truck needs to go from house to house. But I think we could tweak our heaviest Global Transmission with some of their "light learning" and have a transmission that can move the heaviest long haul truck much more efficiently than ever before—and at a lower price point than we've ever offered. Those trucks going across country don't need the same kind of take-off ability the garbage guys do, they just need to be able to sustain that power at the lowest possible price. Because long haul trucking is the biggest segment of mediums and heavies—and the one where Eden continues to eat our lunch—we've got a lot to go after. It would be nice to hit Eden where it hurts the most, for a change, and I think there's a good chance we can do that together.

I understand there will be staff consolidations and I fear we'll lose some good people. Sounds like ZX would keep some or all the engineering here in Westerville—as long as folks only need to fly every once in awhile, not move, to Germany, I think we'll be OK.

Let me know if you need anything else.

[Anniston Email]

From: John Hattley, Anniston Director Sales and Marketing

To: Bobbie Johnson, Anniston President and Grand Vice President

Subject: Confidential—Analysis of Potential Transaction

Bobbie—as you requested, I've talked to my People Transportation and Waste Removal guys (without explaining exactly why) and thought about this ZX takeover myself. Here's what I think.

Part of me is really excited about the possibility. Clink told me all about why he thinks the combination will allow us to better go after the long haul market. I didn't understand all the engineering gobblygook but I can't remember the last time I saw Billy so excited about a new product—and remember how excited he was about the Global Transmission line. If we can finally break Eden's stranglehold on that market, that could be some real big bucks—maybe even more than if the management buyout had worked out?

I kind of expected our bus and garbage guys to be against the deal but they weren't. Maybe they just don't think it's real. The bus guy said he would be excited about "working with my main competitor." The garbage guy said he usually sees them only in the heavy refuse route part of his world, not elsewhere, but respects the heck out them.

Another part of me would be disappointed to see the sale go through, and not just because it might mean that some German takes my job. As you know, we've been fighting them wherever we see them since they came over a few years ago. We put in place the "kill them in the cradle" strategy to try to avoid this day and spent a lot of money on the Global Transmission. Selling out to them makes it seem like all those actions were failures and this old sales guy doesn't like to lose a sale to anybody. But you can't win them all.

So bottomline is that there seems to be a lot of upside to a deal, maybe new sales and maybe even better margins. You can count on me to make it not only work but succeed beyond even the dreams of the Germans.

Johnny H.

Anniston Automatic Division
Strategic Review

Grand Motors Corporation

Presentation to Board of Directors

Kim Sendek, CFO

Summary

- Review started six months ago
  - Keep Anniston Automatic; or
  - Sell to Financial or Strategic Buyer
- Maintaining Anniston less than optimal
  - Not core Grand business
  - Likely need to further invest to meet competition
- Financial buyer offers lower than expected
- Offer from ZX highest and higher than expected
  - Recommend accepting ZX offer

Maintaining Anniston Not Optimal

- Anniston a remnant from earlier strategy to invest in many businesses like refrigerators and locomotives
- Grand makes few medium and no heavy trucks
- Grand has expertise in light vehicles and the very different transmissions in them
- Anniston will continue to require investment, even after Global Transmission
  - Lower cost and improve fuel efficiency to increase automaticity
  - Need to match expected investments by Eden and ZX

Financial Buyer Offers Lower Than Expected

- Two financial buyers participated in process
  - Bane Capital on its own
  - Scylla Capital with Anniston management
- Both bidders offers were below amount needed to make sale optimal
- Neither offered explanation for low bids

Offer From ZX Higher Than Expected

- ZX only strategic buyer to participate in process
- Initial offer 15% higher than better financial buyer offer and 5% above necessary threshold
- Exclusive negotiations and limited due diligence have slightly increased the offer

Potential Ramifications of Sale to ZX

- ZX willing to offer supply agreement for Grand medium trucks
- ZX expected to continue marketing efforts to increase automaticity, both in US and Europe
  - New Global Transmission helpful for both
  - ZX likely to continue to invest in development
- Some pushback possible from customers in certain "heavily automatic" vocations
  - Some played Anniston versus ZX since ZX entry
  - Minority of sales and ZX believes it can manage

Recommendation

- Finalize sale of Anniston Transmission Division to ZX
- Completion of final documents and certain regulatory filings necessary

Project Clifford

Presentation to ZX Board of Directors

Project Clifford Summary

- At Board's direction, have pursued an acquisition of "the big dog" for months
- Entered exclusive negotiations four weeks ago along with some "lite due diligence"
- Process has confirmed initial intelligence
  - Acquisition at price offered is most efficient way to continue to increase automaticity and protect margins both in US and Europe
- Recommend completion of transaction

Potential Synergies – Engineering

- Anniston Global Transmission is impressive line of products with potential to increase automaticity in US and Europe
  - Lightest transmission could be sold in pickups, largest light segment in US
  - Entire product line transferrable to Europe with minimal modifications from ZX Engineering
  - Potential lower cost could make automatics more attractive to new medium and heavy vocations
- Alternative to invest in updated ZX transmissions likely even more expensive than acquisition

Potential Synergies – Marketing

- Combine expertise – and marketing staffs – as try to increase automaticity in US and Europe
  - Especially helpful in US as Eden expected to soon begin selling "automated manual" with easier shifting
- Acquisition would eliminate need to market against Anniston in Europe, expected next year
- Any bus customer complaints manageable

Next Steps

- If Board approves, next steps would be to complete final documentation, due diligence and several regulatory filings